UK500:
Birding in the Fast Lane

James Hanlon

Brambleby Books
Harpenden

UK500: Birding in the Fast Lane
© James Hanlon, 2006

All Rights Reserved

No part of this book may be reproduced in any form by photocopying or by any electronic or mechanical means, including information, storage or retrieval systems, without permission in writing from both the copyright owner and the publisher of this book.

ISBN 0-9543347-8-7
ISBN(13) 9780954334789

Published 2006 by
BRAMBLEBY BOOKS,
Harpenden, UK
www.bramblebybooks.co.uk

Reprinted with corrections, August 2007

Cover design and layout by Creatix Design Services
Front cover photograph by James Hanlon
Back cover photographs by James Hanlon, portrait of author by Elizabeth Noden

Printed in Germany for Brambleby Books by
AZ Druck und Datentechnik GmbH, Kempten

To Mum and Liz

About the Author

James Hanlon was born in South London in December 1974. He settled with his family in the East End in the late 70s, growing up in East Ham, where very early on he developed a keen interest in wildlife, regularly going out bird watching by the age of 10. By his mid-teens, the author had established himself as a keen 'twitcher', contributing illustrations and occasionally photographs to a number of rare bird publications. All the drawings in the present work are by the author.

In July 1996, he graduated from Bangor University with an Honours degree in Zoology with Marine Zoology and a basic understanding of the Welsh language (or at least the words which accompany Welsh road signs). In 1999, he then embarked on a 15-month solo-backpacking trip which saw him hitching around New Zealand in between periods of work, birding and bungee-jumping, before spending six months in Australia. Only when he was left busking on street corners for a bed for the night did he realise it was time to return home via Bali where he spent a fortnight haggling with locals over cheap didgeridoos. Back in the UK, Hanlon returned to twitching and soon decided he would try to record his 500th bird species by his 30th birthday at the end of 2004.

Presently, the author works as an Immigration Enforcement Officer in Essex and lives with his girlfriend near Cambridge. They have a salamander (Scooby) who has just turned 13.

Contents

	Foreword	11
	Introduction	13
Chapter 1	The Ancient Mariner	22
Chapter 2	Pilgrimage to Shetland	27
Chapter 3	Visiting Albert	31
Chapter 4	In the Company of Whales	35
Chapter 5	Southbound to Scilly	40
Chapter 6	October Thrushes	51
Chapter 7	Cape Clear	59
Chapter 8	The Rescue	65
Chapter 9	The Siege	69
Chapter 10	Day Trip to Dingle	73
Chapter 11	Fair Isle's Double	78
Chapter 12	All At Sea	83
Chapter 13	The Final Fling	92
Listings	Bird sightings mentioned in the text	103
Listings	The Big List	109
Resources	Online resources for Birders	124
	Glossary	125
	Acknowledgements	127

Foreword

Birding in the Fast Lane: the new twitching? Watching birds is not a new fascination, but no longer is it the preserve of curates or the elderly. It is now a popular pastime across the board and attracts devotees of all ages. For some though, it can become an obsession, and it takes on a life of its own — so much so that these committed enthusiasts are sectioned off as 'birders'. Birding (or twitching) is a pursuit that can completely possess a young person. Twitching is all about seeing rare birds. The term has occasionally been borrowed by the collectors of bugs and weeds, or even the odd whale, but a real twitcher is a fanatical birder in pursuit of a specific goal: a new bird. It is not like stamp-collecting or train-spotting, mainly because there's absolutely no guarantee that the target object will even be collectable. Birds have wings, and they all too frequently just fly away! Although it is the lot of the avid twitcher to accept such misses (dips), it is a painful experience that is best avoided. Risk management is essential, and there are two factors the modern collector soon realises are of the utmost importance. The first is being in receipt of the information. The second is being available. It is the latter which is the true test of character, because building such an immense degree of spontaneity into one's life requires real dedication. Thanks to 'Birdline' and the various paging systems on offer nowadays, knowing instantly that a 'needed' bird has appeared in Britain is child's play, but it still has to be collected, and here lies the challenge. Getting to some wayward rarity in a hurry can be the most horrendously nerve-wracking experience. Personal relationships can be tested, and so can the cheque book, but the rewards are worth it. Five hundred species by the age of 30, for example! Never mind it has meant being dragged from the Minch by a lifeboat, or having a small piece of ear glued back on after a car crash on the M4, this surely has to be something to be proud of. James Hanlon certainly thinks so, and in the following pages, he shares with us his passion and commitment to birds...and clubbing.

Richard Millington
Birding World
April 2006

Introduction

Why have I written this book? Well, I enjoy telling stories and the endless tales of my quests to see rare birds in the British Isles frequently produce reactions ranging from fascination through varying degrees of incredulity to utter horror on the faces of those listening. 'You did all that for a bird!? You should write a book.' So I did.

It has been said that everyone has a book within them – if only the one about their own personal experiences. The following chapters focus on my birding adventures in the UK and Ireland. By early 2004, I had managed to see almost 500 species and the prospect of reaching this significant number before my 30th birthday encouraged me to step up my efforts by a notch in the autumn of that year. Few people of my generation have achieved this, and I knew it would be a challenge, particularly with a self-imposed deadline. I would have to be prepared to travel anywhere in the British Isles at the drop of a hat. This was nothing new, but if it was a particularly productive autumn, my dedication would be severely tested. My work contract had ended in May though and, for once, I had time on my side.

I have enjoyed looking at birds immensely in other parts of the world but have always been worried that 'world listing' might just 'take over' and I could find myself addicted to the activity of globe-trotting to add to an ever increasing personal list of birds. Unfortunately, as much as I would like this lifestyle, lack of time and money stand in the way. So I've stuck to the odd backpacking trek in which birding has remained a sideline interest rather than the main focus of the trip. This ensures that I do not feel that I have to visit every birding hotspot when I visit a new country. I am always itching to get out in the field but I have rediscovered the art – and pleasure – of finding one's own birds in unknown locations, and the urge to travel vast distances for a few 'ticks' has seldom gripped me once I am outside the British Isles.

Birders get different types of enjoyment from their hobby. I was drawn to the 'twitching' scene in particular, partly because I love the thrill of the chase. These personal accounts are actually more about the chase than the birds themselves. The chase keeps the adrenalin flowing to the point that, in extreme cases, finding the bird becomes almost an anticlimax! You finally clap eyes on whatever avifaunal delight you've been travelling long distances to see, then have to stand back for a few seconds while you recover from all the nail-biting tension that tends to accompany such (sometimes fruitless) trips. The relief can be overwhelming, especially if you have journeyed far, often hundreds of kilometres and at great expense.

Birders are forever getting frustrated at being labelled with the overused tag of 'twitcher' (just ask Bill Oddie). The term is largely one used by the Press, generally when referring to anyone who has so much as glanced at a bird (this happened to Britney Spears not long ago when a journalist got over-excited at seeing a couple of bird pictures on her wall).

Well I *am* a twitcher – and, despite being aware of some of the limitations of my sometimes controversial hobby, I'm proud of it. A twitcher is essentially a birdwatcher who travels to see individual rare birds that have turned up well away from where they should normally be. At its most competitive, twitching can appear to be a bunch of blokes (it tends to be rather male-dominated) trying to outdo each other with an ever-burgeoning list of birds seen or ticked. The essence of twitching is to 'collect' bird sightings, though luckily there is very much more to it than this.

Twitchers (in my experience, and I certainly hope that I am one of these) are usually birders foremost, and 'listers' second. Far from just being interested in the tick, they are usually committed to the pursuit of knowledge in all matters concerned with the occurrence of rare birds: identification, taxonomy, distribution, moult strategy, and migration patterns may all come into the equation when appreciating a rare wind-blown waif. The vast majority of birdwatchers are also concerned with common birds too, particularly their biology and conservation. There can be few twitchers who are unconcerned with the environment. But the thing that makes them tick – quite literally – is the occurrence of these rare birds. And most birdwatchers do, in fact, have an element of 'twitchiness' about them. The birder who goes to see a neighbour because he or she has a tawny owl roosting in the garden has become a twitcher of sorts. And it's not always just birds.

When the doomed Northern Bottle-nosed Whale swam up the River Thames into central London this January (2006), more than 10,000 people lined the bridges and river banks over two days in the hope of glimpsing this rare animal, as many had never before seen a whale. The Press from all over the world converged on what became possibly the largest scale 'twitch' ever. Birders and other wildlife enthusiasts on-site were bemused to see so many members of the public, temporarily at least, showing the sort of curiosity which compels people to travel to see a rare species. Of course, there are a few who are so besotted with the competitive element that the tick, no doubt, does become more important than its context. But as with almost anything, people are drawn to it for different reasons. Good luck to them. The important thing in my opinion is getting some form of enjoyment from birds. How you do that is in the end entirely up to you.

Twitching is a largely harmless pursuit, but the occasional convergence of a large number of people trying to see a bird – which may be elusive, mobile or on private land – has sometimes led to conflicts of interest. The bird-mad enthusiasts may have travelled a great distance and may consider this to be the only chance they'll ever have of seeing this particular species. A code of conduct is required to protect the reputation of birding and minimise any distress to the birds or local residents. In my experience, twitchers are usually very well behaved, but some occasionally get carried away and end up spoiling it for others. As a birder, I rely on the good nature of wardens, landowners and birders who broadcast the discovery of a rare bird. Occasionally, such news of a rarity is 'suppressed' by the person who found it. This may be for a legitimate reason – for example, if the bird in question is on private land with strictly no public access or close to rare breeding species which might desert nests as a result of disturbance. Such suppression of its presence, however, is occasionally out of pure selfishness or ignorance, sometimes borne of a general prejudicial dislike of twitchers. This is always a sad state of affairs as the suppressors may miss out on the opportunity of potentially raising large amounts of money for charity, because such collections are often made at the site of a 'twitch'. Thankfully, the majority of birders like to share their good fortune with others.

How does bird news reach us? The scene has certainly benefited from the Communications Revolution. The use of mobile phones and the Internet has boomed and both are valuable resources for relaying bird news in an expanding market. During the 1960s, bird news tended to arrive by postcard and could be days, if not weeks, old. By the 70s, twitching was taking off and a national grapevine was set up. Nancy's, a small café in the tiny village of Cley on the north Norfolk coast, became the nerve-centre for bird news and people would ring in from all over the country to find out what was around. Nancy's was an institution in its heyday and the quaint village of Cley has remained a birding Mecca. In the mid-80s, a premium rate telephone news service was established there. 'Birdline' proved immensely popular and still runs today. It was set up as part of the Bird Information Service, fronted by two distinguished birders who also started the quality monthly journal *Twitching*, soon afterwards to be renamed *Birding World*.

In the early 90s, pagers were introduced and were soon being operated by two companies specialising in information on scarce migrant and vagrant birds in the UK. Big business had arrived and now pagers are arguably the single most important tool in the field for keeping up to date with bird news. It's never been easier to find out which birds are around, and commercialisation of the market has opened up twitching to a much wider audience that would once have needed to be part of an elite nationwide grapevine to get this kind of news. Text messaging is increasingly popular as is the Internet. It is now possible to find photos of a bird on the worldwide web before you've even set off to see it, as the rising popularity of digital cameras and digi-scoping (where the camera is affixed or held up to a telescope for photography) has ensured that photos can be downloaded and are 'online' within hours of a particular bird's discovery. Pagers tell you not only where the bird is, but also how well it's showing, to the point that you have a fair idea just before you arrive as to whether or not you'll actually see your quarry. Premium rate information lines still run, covering both national and regional information, but are used considerably less than they were during the late 80s when I first entered the scene. CB radios are still used on the Isles of Scilly in October but have now largely been replaced by mobile phones and pagers. Things have come a long way indeed since those first few postcards were circulated.

Chasing rare birds can be simple. It has never been easier to get up-to-the-minute bird news and, when there is a crowd available to show you the bird, you may not even need to search for it yourself. Where's the fun in that? But then everyone has to start somewhere. Of course, with experience, knowledge grows and so does the accrued wisdom known as 'fieldcraft'. It took me years to discover that, with a bit of luck, you can stumble upon these birds yourself. Not all rarities have to be 'twitched' – to a degree, you can find your own. And so I spend most of my time checking local areas; I am one of the scouts, as it were. Most birders do the same, but some spend more time travelling to see other people's discoveries than looking themselves. This way they get to see a fascinating array of birds, the majority of which they will never 'chance upon' themselves because rare birds are, by definition, rare. An Ivory Gull is just another good bird to a twitcher…but to the finder, it's a once-in-a-lifetime discovery – like winning the lottery. Therefore, few birders will ever chance upon their 'own' Ivory Gull. If they want to see one in Britain they will almost certainly have to twitch it. For the record, I've never found an Ivory Gull. In fact, as I live a long way from the coast, I've probably more chance of finding Kylie Minogue on my local patch. Now there's a thought.

This leads me nicely onto my next point. In Britain (and to a lesser extent, Ireland) rare birds are frequently treated like celebrities. Crowds gather upon news of a sighting, and the paparazzi are all after that exclusive shot. Elsewhere, they cause less excitement, but certain countries (most notably Scandanavian countries, Holland and the USA) do have a well-developed twitching scene. Their rarities seldom attract quite the crowds we get in Britain however, which can number hundreds, or even thousands. In 1989, I was one of a crowd of 3,000 people (see plate 1) trying to see Europe's first Golden-winged Warbler, an elusive, blue tit-sized bird which was moving around back gardens on a housing estate. Police had to control the numbers and looked on in astonishment when every now and then a stampede occurred.

Golden-winged Warbler

The physical geography of the United Kingdom and Ireland is such that it supports a rich bird life. It may not have quite the species diversity of some similar-sized tropical countries, but it does have a wealth of habitats and an exceptionally long coastline. Perched off the north-western side of Europe on the edge of the Atlantic, it is in an ideal spot to intercept millions of migrating birds. Most of these will be travelling between northern Europe and Africa but there are others from further afield. Asian species come in from the Far East; Trans-Atlantic vagrants get whisked over in Atlantic weather systems; overshooting migrants arrive in spring from Africa, way north of their usual Mediterranean breeding grounds; ocean-going seabirds from as far away as the Southern Hemisphere end up touring our coastline. Of the small proportion of these rare migrants which actually get discovered on our soil, over our waters, or in our airspace (and there's little doubt that the majority go unnoticed), there can be quite a welcoming committee of birders eager for a glimpse.

One criticism frequently made of the twitching fraternity is that the tick (of a new bird on one's list) is the driving factor for any birding expedition. Everyone is different of course, but I defy anyone to find a birder who is interested solely in ticking off a list. Virtually every birder I have ever met takes pleasure from working a local patch and twitching birds that do not provide ticks of any description. And very few birders are willing to clap eyes on something and then leave straight away. A bird is there to be enjoyed – its behaviour, plumage and character are to be savoured, discussed (sometimes hotly debated), described in detail, photographed, sketched, reported. This simply wouldn't happen if everyone watching the bird did so only to add it to their list.

A trip to the Shetland Islands can cost hundreds of pounds sterling, especially if a charter flight is arranged at short notice and yet for not much more than that, one could have a holiday outside Europe and see dozens of new birds. So the 'tick' can be important, and it is clear that this side of birding can lead to some pretty irrational behaviour. Forking out for a long distance trip for a bird one has already seen in a far-flung distant land, perhaps many times, is one example of such behaviour. But there is a different 'feel' to seeing that bird in a British context. Especially if, despite its abundance abroad, it is a great rarity here, maybe even being recorded for the very first time. Yet the list is not just a collection of bird names. It is a representation of a birder's hobby, signifying the hours of enjoyment of watching birds, poring over books and journals, searching every kind of habitat in an effort to encounter some of the many bird species that grace this planet. Going hand-in-hand with every tick is a unique personal experience, a new file of knowledge, an opportunity to familiarise oneself with that particular bird. Observation of a rarity represents a personal involvement in, and appreciation of, the unique ornithological occurrence of a vagrant bird from a foreign land. Thus the tick is important, but it is the experience that is the real prize.

The size of a list does not indicate how good a birder you are, but does show, to some extent, your level of involvement with birds. A list is simply an arbitrary product of the human desire for order (as one birder once accurately stated on TV). It is a human interpretation of a world created outside the existence of boundaries. It lists birds as 'species' but the classification of a species is fundamentally flawed, mainly because speciation is always in progress amongst populations of all organisms – and studying gene flow in wild populations is a notoriously difficult process. Different species can be very similar and it is difficult to know where to draw the line of specific division, where to whack down the point of no return where two populations have become so genetically isolated – either through reproductive/genetic or geographic means, or both – that any further free gene transfer does not generally occur. But we humans always attempt to draw the line somewhere so that we can recognise each

Introduction

bird as a classifiable entity. This is one of the debates that troubles many birders – and taxonomists in other fields. However, to examine this more philosophical side of birding too closely would be to stray beyond the realms of this book. It does, however, serve to undermine the whole idea of listing, which some would say is fundamental to the birding experiences they enjoy.

It is very easy to become sucked in to the competitiveness of listing. The UK400 Club, run by Lee Evans, publishes the UK and Irish lists of those who have seen more than 400 species, along with listing guidelines*. This has increased competitiveness among birders to the extent that at times it seems to be a case of 'keeping up with the Jones's'. It is hard to resist keeping track of what your list 'neighbour' has seen and, even outside the UK400 Club, groups of friends often compete, trying to outdo each other with the size of their lists. Sometimes I feel that the competitiveness can draw focus away from what unites us all in the first place – the love of birds. I too was fascinated by Lee's lists and still find they arouse my curiosity. The idea of listing sometimes makes me feel I am being drawn away from the love of birds themselves – yet still it draws me in. It is a warning sign however, when you feel that you are going for a bird because you have to rather than because you want to. Or if you worry more about the birds you have missed, than take pleasure in the birds you have seen.

I have chosen a selection of my more memorable days out chasing rarities for the main part of this book and have included a glossary as the world of birding offers a startling array of new words to the English language. So if I were to start talking about a 'megamover', or appreciating a bird's 'jizz' whilst getting 'stonking' views through one's 'bins', I hope that I won't lose you. To leave out the jargon of birding culture just wouldn't be right, although in truth, I have tried to minimise such jargon in the text.

---

* These are the guidelines I have used for the purpose of this book. Some may criticize this decision as they include some birds not counted on the official scientifically-recognized list. Even so, many birders agree that they are a more user-friendly alternative.

One final point. Driving long distances for birds on little sleep is not without personal risk. Most birders I refer to in this book have been doing this for years and have some idea of their limitations, but no one is invincible. Birders occasionally become carried away with getting to a bird quickly, but in the end safety comes first ... or certainly should do. No bird is worth an injury, let alone a life. When I talk about 'putting my foot down', it is always relative and done with caution and respect for other road-users. Even when I'm after a Siberian Rubythroat!

The Ancient Mariner

My mission, should I have chosen to accept it – which I did – was to travel to an island in the Bristol Channel. Here I was to attempt to gain visual contact with a small seabird from the North Pacific. Sounds easy doesn't it? Little did I realise however that fate would be placing some serious obstacles in my path and that my dedication was to receive a real test.

On the 14th April 1991, I phoned Birdline, the rare bird information line, which was a lifeline to birders until the introduction of pagers for such news a few months later. There was nothing unusual about my decision to call – I phoned regularly to keep up to date with what was around. However, I was about to experience a feeling I had never felt before, and rarely since. I was being told that the Ancient Murrelet had returned to Jenny's Cove on the Isle of Lundy. This is a bird which had been found in May 1990 and had last been seen a month later in late June. During this time I'd been frantically trying to arrange a trip to go and see it, but was not having much luck, as I was still dependent on birders with cars giving me a lift. By the time I did get a lift, the bird had not been reported for a week and a half. It was such a special bird though and I had been going through so much agony during the preceding weeks, I was willing to try anything. What happened? I went, put more effort into searching Jenny's Cove auk by auk than I have ever put into a whole month's birding, 'dipped', got lost in the fog, significantly delaying the boat while a search party was set up, and finally, double-dipped on the way home when missing the (football) World Cup final.

The reason for my desperation to see the bird? Let me tell you about the Ancient Murrelet. It is a species of auk from the North Pacific and tends to avoid the high Arctic, so it had actually come from the other side of the world to get here, undertaking, it would seem, not just a trans-Atlantic crossing, but quite a substantial overland one too – quite a feat for a tiny seabird more used to life on the open ocean. This makes it one of the least likely birds on the British list ever to make it here again. No wonder it was a first for the Western Palaearctic (this term is widely used in birding to cover the geographical region of Europe, North Africa and the Middle East). But it wasn't just the extreme rarity of the bird or where it came from. There was some other attraction – its appearance, its habits (mainly nocturnal for a start) made it to me a beautiful and truly enigmatic creature, considerably more aesthetically appealing than many of the smaller plain-looking birds I had travelled to see. I was also at that age (16) when everything seems just that bit more important than it really is. This youthful enthusiasm, the passion of adolescence, was forever leading me to believe that there would never again be a chance to see certain birds. In the vast majority of cases, this wasn't the case – as I was subsequently to learn. 'It'll come again,' many a wise birder would nod knowingly in my direction on seeing my angst at missing some rarity or other. They had seen it all before of course.* But the Murrelet was different and I knew that it would be a very long wait until the next one arrived, if it ever did. In the UK at least, it really is a once-in-a-lifetime bird. Anyway, it was without doubt my most wanted bird on the British list. I was so desperate to see one; I vowed one day to travel to its homeland in the Aleutians or the Pribilof Islands.

---

* I myself can't believe that once, when in my teens, I headed to North Ronaldsay in the Orkney Isles for a rustic bunting, reaching as far as Aberdeen from my London home, before turning back on 'negative news'. This bird is actually a regular visitor and I have now seen several, including one a few months later in my home county of Greater London.

Meanwhile, I struggled to come to terms with the fact that I had missed the species in Britain, – but this gap on my list haunted me. I kept hoping it would return the following year, really believing it would at times. No one else shared my optimism however and, as the 1991 birding calendar got into full swing, I gradually began to accept that it would never return.

That is why I experienced such a strange feeling when I heard the Birdline message on April 14th. As I learned of those magic words, adrenalin surged through me and the message suddenly seemed to play in slow motion. My dream had come true. When I eventually came to my senses and realised I wasn't dreaming I set to work instantly to get myself on a trip to see it. I arranged to go with my mother the following weekend, but also got myself booked for two other carloads for some time in the near future – 'reserve' trips, just to be on the safe side.

The first blow was a cruel and painful one. As we headed west amongst heavy traffic on the M4 somewhere near Bristol, there was a sudden slowing of the cars ahead. Suddenly we were braking and then skidding into the outside lane. There was a 'bang' as we were hit by an overtaking car before careering into the central reservation. I looked down. Blood had dripped onto my cream jumper, a personal favourite. There was intense pain in the side of my head where something had hit me. My mother had a minor facial injury but was more worried by the fact that blood appeared to be coming from inside my ear. We were helped across to the hard shoulder to await an ambulance.

A couple of hours later we left the hospital, a small piece of my ear having been surgically glued back into place. It had seemed that in terms of seeing this bird, we were well and truly 'up the creek without a paddle', or somewhere similar. The car had been written off and so had some of my optical equipment (the telescope was in a terrible state and the tripod was beyond repair). But we were not going to let one little setback stop us from seeing our bird. To my surprise, my mother offered me the option of continuing. Then again, we didn't have much time to catch the next train. The police who had escorted us to the hospital realised this and kindly raced us to the railway station in a patrol car with flashing lights and sirens. Unfortunately, we narrowly missed our train but there was one soon afterwards which would take us most of the way, as far as Taunton, which for now would have to do.

Chapter 1

After the train journey was a 100-km taxi journey which cost a painful £60. But finally we made it to our guest house in Ilfracombe, from which the boat would sail merrily to Lundy in the morning and I would skip gaily up to Jenny's Cove and see the Murrelet. Once on the island, the chances of seeing the bird were high and surely nothing could stop us getting to Lundy now. Or could it?

The following morning I was in a good mood as I headed for the quay. This soon wore off though when the boat didn't sail on time. In fact, as time wore on, the situation became painfully clear: the boat was not going to sail. Whether or not it was a technical problem I was not sure, but it was final and therefore the cause of the cancellation was largely irrelevant. We would have to return next week in order to get to Lundy. We had overcome all odds to make it this far, yet it had all been in vain. There followed what must have sounded like the dialogue from an episode of the Osbournes, on one of Ozzy's worst days. For a while, I channelled my 'youthful enthusiasm' into conjuring up a suitable volley of expletives. If language really can be colourful, there was a magnificent rainbow over the quay at Ilfracombe that morning.

This bird was not playing ball. Or at least fate wasn't. A few days later came my next attempt when I travelled with Lee Evans. It was my first weekday trip. Maybe it would bring me more luck. I certainly hoped so as I boarded Lundy's passenger ferry, the *MS Oldenburg*, during the early hours of the 24th April. Had I had the lungs of a sperm whale I most certainly would have held my breath during the next couple of hours. It was a tense time and a lot was resting on this trip. Once on the island, I marched up to Jenny's Cove mainly in silence, praying that the mission would be a successful one.

I have to admit now, it was a bit of an anti-climax. I saw the bird on arrival. But I actually felt a little unimpressed with the rather distant views and, as it was still extremely early and I had had little sleep, I found it hard to feel overly joyous. Here I was, tired and hungry and watching a small bird half a kilometre away. It was great to see it but it had become such a big thing in my mind, that an anti-climax was almost inevitable. Looking back now, it seems perhaps that this was an early lesson in keeping things in perspective. Seeing that bird really had been a major ambition, and although I felt immense relief as I watched this strange creature lazing

25

about halfway up a cliff on the far side of the cove, it seemed hard to appreciate that this really was what I had waited for all this time (see plate 8). A tiny auk, much smaller than a neighbouring Razorbill, with a noticeable white stripe above the eye, grey upperparts, mainly black head and white below. It rested horizontally and looked rather awkward when moving (and positively reptilian in the opinion of some other onlookers). An amazing bird to see in Britain, but it was just a bird and a distant one at that. Disappointed by the range at which we were watching it, I was actually one of the first to leave. The Tavern apparently served a cracking good breakfast, and I could feel a Homer Simpson attack coming on. Nothing eats quite like a growing teenage boy (Homer aside) and it wasn't long before I was stuffing my face.

Years later, I can reflect on how the pursuit of rare birds can be an emotional affair, but when it is the thrill of the chase that drives you, there are highs and lows. There is always a certain 'buzz' from connecting with a rarity, but it wears off quickly. Some people are drawn to this part of twitching more than others; it is a very different experience to the gentle pastime of appreciating everyday birds in their natural environment, and I can see why some birdwatchers don't get involved. Who would choose stress over relaxation? Someone who enjoys the buzz of seeing a new bird and can't get enough, that's who. Guilty as charged, but I don't really have any regrets, just a wealth of fond memories. Seeing the Ancient Murrelet is one – in fact, to me, it proved a major accomplishment, but never again will seeing a single bird matter quite that much.

The Murrelet was not only present throughout much of the spring of 1991, it actually re-appeared the following year too, giving many more people the option of journeying to see this unusual bird. I believe several thousand made the pilgrimage. It turned out that I was not the only person injured en route to Lundy either. I heard some time later that a friend of mine had actually lost his thumb when it was crushed between the boat and the quay whilst disembarking. Ouch! When you carry on even when your hobby is costing you body parts, you know you are a dedicated soul. And here was me thinking the Ancient Murrelet had cost me a lot. Well, this chapter is dedicated to you, Chris 'The Thumb'. It seems birding isn't always quite as safe as one might think.

Chapter 2

Pilgrimage to Shetland

At the very 'top' of Britain lies a cluster of islands collectively known as the Shetland Islands. The Shetlands are so far north that most maps of the British Isles have to squeeze them into a box just off the Scottish coast, and hence few people realize just how isolated they really are. The islands have a real Norse feel – the Viking invasions which began in the eighth century had a lasting influence on the dialect, customs and music of Shetland's residents, even though the islands were claimed by Scotland in the fifteenth century. The area is not only rich in natural history but also in human history – the legacy of 5,000 years of continual habitation in an area littered with archaeological remains which have often been left relatively undisturbed thanks to the non-intensive, unobtrusive style of farming that prevails. Visitors come here to appreciate many aspects of Shetland, from its rich, cultural heritage and folk music to its windswept hills and famous seabird colonies.

To many, the Shetlands are the ultimate test of dedication when it comes to UK twitching. Because of their geographic location and relative isolation, they receive an impressive number of rarities, but be warned – travelling to Shetland is not cheap. Birders can spend many hundreds of pounds getting there for a rare bird (especially if flying from an airport in the south) and it is not unknown for the more dedicated ones to make two trips within the space of a few days if the first is unsuccessful. Unlike the Isles of Scilly, Shetland is a sprawling mass of an archipelago, stretching for well over 150km, and providing a valuable resting spot for tired migrants from the east, particularly during the months of May, September and October. There are occasionally rarer birds mixed in, and a period of prolonged easterly winds can be particularly productive. Its scarcity of vegetation often helps to concentrate lost and migrating birds into areas of cover, such as the gardens in some parts of the main town, Lerwick. And it is Lerwick that became temporary home to a Pine Grosbeak for a month during the early part of 1992. Having never twitched this 'ultimate' birding destination, it was with a great deal of excitement and trepidation that I headed north in late March '92.

It was a gruelling journey from the start – a 12-hour coach trip followed by a long anxious day spent in Aberdeen, wondering why there was no news on my quarry, the Pine Grosbeak. It was a suitably rare bird – just the tenth ever recorded in Britain and the first for around 17 years. Eventually news of its continued presence broke while I was at the station and the trip was thus still on. A young tripod-toting man in the coffee shop there was not a birder as I discovered much to my embarrassment when I went over to talk to him; so I was still on my own. I did however meet seven other birders on the boat – all with excuses for not going sooner with the main crowds, such as 'You can't take off instantly with a wife and kids y'know'.

By the following morning – and bear in mind it is a 14-hour crossing – I was feeling decidedly green after a rather greasy breakfast. Not only seasick, but envious as hell of those who could afford to fly, thus avoiding seasickness. Still, on green issues, I did my bit for the environment with a touch of recycling afterwards when I let the sea enjoy the breakfast I couldn't keep down – and then felt decidedly less green.

Arrival in Lerwick was amidst a kind of sleety hail – this really did feel like another country – and I was surprised to see a thin covering of snow, blanketing vast areas of ground. As the weather improved, I marched through Lerwick, feeling rather uncomfortable with sodden feet but soon found the spot the bird frequented. As the sun appeared, the snow began to melt, creating myriads of rivulets running down the street, all making straight for my Nike Air Cross trainers. It was amazing how quickly the snow had disappeared and by the afternoon the ground was bone-dry. During this time I had managed to see a young Iceland Gull and nearly broke my arm, slipping on a wet grassy slope by the roadside. But what of the Grosbeak?

After an agonising six-and-a-half hour wait, a local birder pulled up with news of its rediscovery. Although a visiting Norfolk birder had claimed to have seen it a few hours earlier just by the hospital, this claim had been dismissed by most after a thorough search of the area. Now though, not only was it showing, it was apparently so close to its observers, that optics were neither necessary nor practical as they wouldn't focus close enough.

I ran so fast I tired at the bottom of the hill and could barely manage the rest. The sight of a group of birders peering into a small garden hedge at point blank range was enough to produce a final spurt of energy and I arrived utterly exhausted. It was 2.50pm and I was standing less than two metres from a gentle-looking bird which bore little resemblance to what I had expected. In those days, I used the *Shell Field Guide to the Birds of Britain & Ireland* for identification. The *Shell Guide* was in a class of its own. It was my Bible. No other British field guide could touch it. But just occasionally it failed to capture the character or 'jizz' of a bird. The trouble with the picture of the Pine Grosbeak in the *Shell Guide* (and make no mistake that, generally speaking, the illustrations in this book are of an exceptionally high standard, probably better than those in any other field guide of the time of its publication in 1980) is that it looks tough. It looks mean. If it could talk it would be saying 'your name's not down mate, you're not coming in' because this bird is clearly the bouncer of the Scandanavian forests. And of course there is its colour. Pink or green evidently. But the bird I was looking at was grey, with an orange head and broad white fringes on the feathers of its wings (see plate 8). Strangely, it didn't have the 'you looking at my pine cone?' scowl, evident in the *Shell Guide* picture. It is actually, in my opinion, a nice surprise to gain a completely different impression of a bird in the flesh as it makes you feel as if you've *really* seen it. (An even better feeling is to clap eyes on a bird you've never even seen in a book – I managed this once or twice in my teens by deliberately not looking in a field guide when going for an exceptionally rare bird, such as a British 'first'). Even the Grosbeak's call seemed not to fit the book's description, sounding more like a strangled budgie to me. It was sitting, mostly quietly, deep in a thick garden hedge but after some time began to feed on buds. It then bounced along a wall and fluttered weakly into another nearby bush and out of view. After what had been an agonisingly long wait, it was smiles all round.

The boat was delayed for 21 hours on my return journey, and I must have spent 50 hours aboard it during the four days it took to get on and off Shetland. That was four days off sixth form college. Perhaps this contributed in a very small way to my poor GCE 'A'-level results the following year. Then again, Pine Grosbeak remains one of my ultimate 'blockers' as this bird has been the only truly 'twitchable' one to turn up in the UK. Even in those days, and as far as I am concerned, I felt I had my priorities right!

Chapter 3

Visiting Albert

Few birds fire the imagination more than the Albatross. Steeped in myth and legend, albatrosses have inspired and fascinated seafarers and birdwatchers for centuries. Spending a large proportion of their life at sea, they roam the open oceans for hundreds of kilometres with scarcely a wing-beat, feeding on squid and sometimes fish, and excreting salt from ingested seawater through neat little tubular glands on their bill. It is a sad fact that around 100,000 of these splendid birds die every year (that's one every five minutes) when they get caught on longline fishing hooks. This has prompted Birdlife International and the RSPB to launch a high profile campaign to 'Save the Albatross'. With 19 of the 21 species of albatross threatened worldwide with extinction, it is certainly a worthwhile cause, especially as the number of fatalities would plummet with a few simple changes in commercial fishing practices.

The wingspan of the largest species nearly touches three and a half metres – a real record-breaker – and they are also known for their touching courtship displays and their habit of mating for life. Most of the world's albatrosses are confined to the Southern Hemisphere but, as with other seabirds, they are highly nomadic and occasionally get sighted in the northern oceans. One species – the Black-browed Albatross – is seen almost annually in British waters, usually from a boat or when passing a remote headland during strong onshore winds. It is surely the ultimate prize for the dedicated seawatching birder. Seeing an Albatross in Britain hasn't always been simply down to luck, however. In 1967, an individual appeared in the gannet colony on Bass Rock, off the Scottish east coast. It returned for the breeding season over the next two years before relocating to Hermaness, at the northernmost tip of Unst (the northernmost island in the Shetland chain) in 1972. It missed a couple of years in the late 80s but other than that was available every year subsequently, until Albert – as the bird became affectionately known, later identified as female, had 'his' last season in 1995 and thereafter disappeared.

1993 was a big year for me. It was the year I started university following my A-levels. Going to Shetland was one trip I had been looking forward to for some time and I was very excited when the news I had been waiting for broke one day on the pager. I journeyed initially by train – a 12-hour trip to Aberdeen. Like any other teenager, I found myself unable to last more than two minutes on public transport without the comfort of my personal stereo blasting out (in my case) hypnotic, trance-inducing dance music at top volume. By the time I had arrived at Aberdeen, my eardrums had melted, or at least partly corroded.

It was several kilometres from the centre of Aberdeen to the airport. I caught the flight without incident and soon found myself on Shetland Mainland, heading from the main airport at Sumburgh to the smaller one, 40 kilometres to the north at Tingwall. It was here though, that things started to go wrong. It is a tiny airport with few staff around. I was the only passenger there and waited patiently but there was no sign of the plane leaving and no real explanation as to its delay. It became doubtful whether I would get to Hermaness that day.

Eventually I was in the air with the pilot in a tiny plane. We were not bound for Unst though – we were returning to Sumburgh. A big mix-up had left various flights delayed or cancelled, and we were on our way to pick up more Unst hopefuls. That was one taxi journey well and truly wasted. Once in the air and Unst-bound, I knew I still had a challenge ahead of me, since reaching Hermaness and thence finding accommodation would not be easy. Locating exactly where Saito Outcrop was at the Hermaness Nature Reserve would be the biggest hurdle. I hung around the airport for some time, watching the oil rig workers, but eventually trundled off to find a place to stay for the night. I struck lucky at the first house I came to. Although there was no sign up, yes, the lady would give me bed and breakfast and an evening meal. I then secured a lift part of the way to Hermaness that took me past Britain's most northerly post office. Soon after that I was crossing bleak moorland in the direction of the cliffs at Hermaness, Britain's most northerly nature reserve, but there was no sign of the albatross that evening. As dusk descended, I began the weary two-and-a-half-hour trudge back to my digs in Baltasound, kept company by various hedgehogs along the route. I was, at this point, Britain's most northerly exhausted and pissed-off person.

The next day saw my return to the cliffs with renewed optimism. The wind was up and the weather generally less settled. A lone Red-throated Diver on a small pool watched as I picked my way towards it. It called once before taking off, inspecting me briefly as it flew close by. Bonxies (Great Skuas) loomed threateningly nearby and, at the cliff-top, a number of Arctic Puffins allowed a close approach. A few Ravens wheeled around and the odd Ring Ouzel put in an appearance, whilst offshore the stacks of Muckle Flugga stood on guard like sentinels as seabirds whizzed past in every direction. Welcome to Hermaness Nature Reserve.

My chances looked remote. The 200m cliffs are some of the highest in Britain, and I was not sure where to start looking. I ventured close to the edge several times, searching through the white dots peppering the cliff-face. These were Northern Gannets and it was with them that the albatross had decided to set up home. Eventually my binoculars ('bins' in birders' terms) settled on what appeared to be a Great Black-backed Gull sitting with the Gannets far below. I tried to steady my hands in the brisk wind and, no, it couldn't be... I dashed back to my 'scope and there 'he' was – 'Mr Albert Ross' in all 'his' magnificent glory (see plate 9). I could barely believe my eyes and was buzzing with excitement. What a magical bird. It was sitting where the Gannets were slightly thinner on the ground, a few yards from a denser group, covering what was presumably Saito Outcrop. Just a shade larger than its neighbours, the 'Ross' sported a large pinkish-yellow bill and a distinctive dark 'brow' through the eye. The back, wings and tail were all a dark grey, almost black, and the bird also had, as I noticed, very large pinkish-grey feet. The poor creature was displaying to the Gannets, occasionally bobbing and swaying its head slightly. It approached one, opening its vast wings and the Gannet, obviously unimpressed, promptly flew off.

I whiled away the rest of the trip, searching unsuccessfully for otters (*Lutra lutra*) and attempting to identify Shetland's avifauna from the bus back to Lerwick. The whole trip had cost me in the region of £400 (nearly two months' wages from my Saturday job at a local supermarket). It had taken several days and it had left me physically exhausted. But I had come away with one of the great prizes of the British 'rare bird scene'. I was one of the few people who had ever seen a real live Albatross in Britain, but as it proved, it was to be my last successful long distance twitch for some time.

The next bird trip was just over a week later to Northern Ireland for a White's Thrush. Once again I journeyed alone, catching the train to Holyhead, the ferry to Dublin and another train from Dublin to Belfast. Here I caught a taxi to the coast, where a small boat took me out to Copeland Island. Several birders who disembarked on the mainland side told me that they had seen the bird an hour and a half previously. I had no support searching for it as everyone else had left, and it was never seen again. Threatened with eviction on my return home, due to my increasingly desperate birding habit, I thought long and hard on that protracted journey back to my home in London. It was more than two years before I attempted a journey of that magnitude for a bird again. Luckily I missed comparatively little in the way of national rarities, and it gave me enough space and money to enjoy student life without having to dash off constantly after new potential ticks. After all, birding isn't everything!

Chapter 4

In the Company of Whales

Certain birds stand high on the list of 'most wanted' and, up until the late 1980s, the Blue-cheeked Bee-eater was one such bird. A resplendent emerald-green visitor, breeding from Morocco to India and wintering south of the Sahara, there surely can be few prizes in birding that can match finding one of these exotic beauties. Then, in 1989, someone did just that in East Yorkshire, and the bird remained in the vicinity long enough to be twitched by the masses. Being then quite young and not in the habit of dashing off after everything, I was not amongst the lucky ones. As it proved, I had a long wait on my hands, but eventually, in 1997, another bird was sighted. It wasn't in a particularly accessible location, nor was it always easy to see. The morning of the 27th June saw half a dozen or so birders, including me, assemble at Aberdeen airport, all nervously hoping to be able to connect with the eighth Blue-cheeked Bee-eater ever recorded in these islands.

Teaming up with my friend Adrian Webb in a hired Ford Fiesta, I soon embarked on a weekend on Shetland which I will not forget in a hurry. Adrian and several other birders had already travelled up from the south of England to pay homage but had returned home without success. This was their second trip. The Bee-eater was at a place called Asta House and luckily this time it proved much easier to see – in fact we saw it before the car had even ground to a halt – and 'crippling' views were enjoyed at a range of about 15 metres. Wow – what a stunner! (see plate 9). A little larger than a Blackbird and bright emerald-green all over, relieved only by blue sides to the face, a black mask and russet throat. We even heard it call and enjoyed some brief flight views. The plumage was sensational – and what a superb setting to be watching it in – much more dramatic than a field edge in north-east England where the last one had set up home. But impressive though the bird was, there were others to see. In fact a total of no less than three potential 'lifers' had lured me here and I felt that already we were on a roll.

Next on the agenda was a long-staying and well-travelled Black Kite on the island of Yell. It was lucky we left when we did – half a second earlier and we may have had a golf ball through the windscreen whilst driving past a course. As it turned out, the maverick little sphere bounced between us and the car in front, a few minutes after we had left Asta House. Shetland was clearly a potentially dangerous place. We journeyed north through magnificent, yet strangely barren, terrain – moorland and rolling hills with countless 'voes' (sheltered inlets) and endless rocky shores – keeping a careful eye out for flying golf balls. Then, as we waited for the ferry, an otter popped up just a few metres from the queuing cars and entertained us for a while.

Black Kite

I love otters. I had seen them for the first time the previous year on the west coast of Scotland after they had eluded me for many years. When I was finally lucky enough to see one, there were in fact three of them – just like the London buses. This particular animal seemed rather unconcerned by the nearby queue of cars – behaviour that is in complete contrast to the exceptionally elusive otters of the southern counties of England which are only reported slightly more often than the Loch Ness Monster and the 'Beast of Bodmin Moor'.

It was a short drive to Setter Farm on Yell where the kite had been residing for some time. Black Kite, a large dark raptor common throughout the continent and indeed much of the world, is a regular visitor to Britain mainly in the spring. Most records are of brief fly-overs, birds which are rarely, if ever seen again; such birds are notoriously difficult to catch up with. This one could not have surrendered itself in more style, giving fantastic views at ranges of often not more than 100 metres or so. At one stage we drove up to the farm to search for it and saw it fly up not 15 metres away. It was almost constantly on view, allowing me to take a rather detailed description of a creature that was basically, well, big and brown. As often happens on Shetland, we had the bird pretty much to ourselves, although Britain's most famous birdwatcher Bill Oddie and his film crew were there when we returned the following day. They were not really after the rarities but couldn't resist popping in to pay their respects (to the bird at least). On this occasion we left with the kite, following it south for a short distance as it drifted high overhead, whilst being mobbed by the occasional Arctic Tern. On an ironic and rather sad note, we had joked about using a dead sheep as bait to lure the kite closer to the road. Shortly after leaving the site, we hit an especially woolly-headed one which strayed in front of the car as we were doing about 60mph. It was, alas, killed instantly, and who knows, maybe the kite later benefited from this poor animal's misfortune. Then again, there were so many dead sheep around, it was probably spoilt for choice. And the car? Amazingly, not a scratch on it. Perhaps all that wool protected it (not so the sheep, obviously).

Three new birds in a day would have been nice, but the Black-headed Bunting on Fetlar was conspicuous by its absence. I knew the dream of a hat-trick was over, though it was nice to visit Fetlar and pay our respects to the delightful Red-necked Phalaropes which breed there. However, as I occasionally reminded myself, listing isn't the be-all and end-all, and it was time to savour the other birds and wildlife present. The following day played host to one of my most memorable sights ever, when a family pod of four Killer Whales (*Orcinus orca*) put in an appearance close to our ferry boat between Yell and Shetland Mainland. We so nearly missed them! Thanks are really due to the boatmen who spotted the magnificent creatures and knocked on all the car windows to let everyone know. They even stopped the boat's engine so we could watch the whales for a little longer. I lapped up every second, as this was one of the most magical natural sights that I have ever witnessed before or since and I was truly privileged to be there. I think, at that point, I felt like I had won the lottery, but it wasn't over yet; the following day produced further cetacean bonanzas off Sumburgh Head, the southern tip of mainland Shetland. A single Minke Whale (*Balaenoptera acutorostrata*) and one, or perhaps two, distant pods of dolphins all put in an appearance, in addition to the usual scattering of Harbour Porpoises occasionally breaking the surface of a sunlit, millpond-like sea. I struggled with the identification of what was little more than a bunch of distant dorsal fins at that range, but checking the field guides later confirmed my suspicions that they were most likely to have been White-beaked Dolphins (*Lagenorhynchus albirostris*).

The funniest moment of the weekend occurred on our final night when I was driving our hired car to Sumburgh Airport at about 2am. I had taken over because Adrian was totally shattered, and we knew that it would be safer for me to complete the final leg of the journey. We had been sleeping in the car all weekend, but at least I hadn't had to bother with the driving so far. As I neared the airport, I negotiated a bend in fits of laughter. Adrian, partially awoken from a semi-comatose state of delirium brought on by extreme exhaustion, had had a brief panic attack as he went to grab a phantom steering wheel in front of him that wasn't there. He had obviously seen the approaching bend and felt that he was still driving. Unable to cope with the complications of consciousness, he immediately relapsed back into his 'zombified' state. The incident still brings a smile to my face even now.

Our bird log for the weekend had been exceptional – Blue-cheeked Bee-eater, Black Kite, King Eider, Icterine Warbler, Red-backed Shrike, and four or five breeding pairs of Red-necked Phalaropes provided the highlights. However, the weekend had been all the more remarkable for the other wildlife we had seen, including three new (to me) mammals I certainly hadn't been expecting. Seeing such fascinating animals is every bit as rewarding as seeing a new bird, and these days I am quite a keen 'mammal twitcher' too, so the weekend really was a resounding success. I was still going over those amazing sightings in my head when I arrived back at my home in Wales after a long drive down from Aberdeen, which included a stop off to see the long-staying Spanish Sparrow in Cumbria, late in the evening of the 30th June. Just before I pulled in off the road something very small darted under the wheels. It looked like a shrew. Investigation of the unfortunately deceased creature confirmed this suspicion, and it was surprisingly small. It looked like a Pygmy Shrew

(*Sorex minutus*) but could have been a young Common Shrew (*S. araneus*). I kept the body, which bore little obvious damage, for analysis. Much as I had always wanted to see a Pygmy Shrew, this was not the circumstance I wished to see it under and I would much rather its life had been spared. It was a few weeks before I was able to test my theory but eventually, with a text book in one hand and tape measure in the other, confirmed that the tiny animal was indeed a 'Pygmy' – at that time, the only one I had ever seen.

Southbound to Scilly

Throughout the years, birding has remained my main hobby of choice. But I do have other interests and, like most young adults, enjoy a good night out and love music. Unfortunately, birding does not always mix well with 'arrangements', 'a social life' and 'other interests'. When they are forced to mix, it can be tricky holding everything together. One year, a Common Yellowthroat on the Isles of Scilly threw my plans for a night out clubbing into complete disarray, as I tried to fit everything in and end up with the bird.

At the risk of going off on an almighty tangent here, let me tell you about the club scene. Clubbing has been another serious hobby of mine. These days my taste in music is broad, but as a teenager I only really had time for dance music – not the cheesy chart tunes, but underground house, garage, jungle, hardcore, trance, ambience…the list goes on. When I fazed somewhat from birding in 1993, my energy and interest had to be channelled elsewhere and I discovered the rave scene. I remember when the parties first hit the headlines (while I was still at school and too young to join the movement) and the tabloids went mad with sensationalism. Of course such parties were frowned upon, being dubbed simply 'drug parties', but there was more to it than that. The disillusioned youth of the Thatcher years had found a collective identity and staged nothing short of a musical revolution; dance music was here to stay and it quickly moved into the mainstream. Instead of driving through the night to distant rarities, I now preferred to dance it away in some obscure field or barn with a bunch of mad-for-it 'crusties' and an illegal sound system, or head off to a huge club night followed by a warehouse party somewhere, or perhaps even one of the giant commercial open-air events where the atmosphere was electric, and you could rub shoulders with 25,000 feel-good nutters jammed into a couple of giant marquees.

It was the perfect place to escape from reality and the pressures of modern day life. I had a fierce passion for the music and was able to completely empty my mind when dancing to it, losing myself in another world. It was a great scene to be part of, and if my parents had the swinging 60s, then the mid-90s was my time. Their generation had Woodstock, mine had Tribal Gathering. To me, it was deeply inspirational and paved the way for my subsequent interest in song-writing and recording. My first ever trip to legendary Liverpool club Cream in 1994 was a particularly inspiring night and it was the reason I wanted to return in 1997 to this amazing venue. By this time, I was growing out of the club scene but I was nevertheless determined to be at Cream's fifth birthday bash.

This event would take place on the 10th/11th October, just about the worst weekend possible for a birder. This is the weekend most head off for the Isles of Scilly, or simply 'Scilly' amongst birders, but for once, birding was to take second place. I really wanted to go to this party. I just prayed no major rarities would turn up. Unfortunately, the gods were having none of it. They whisked a Yellowthroat off the east coast of North America and deposited it unceremoniously on the island of St Mary's for the visiting hordes to discover, which they duly did on the 9th October. If I went to Liverpool I wouldn't be on the islands until the 11th or 12th.

I had to take the risk as I had tickets to this event, for myself and others. I left work early on the 10th and headed for the North-West. My first stop was Bangor, and it took no less than eight hours (a personal record; it would normally take five to six hours) to get there. The traffic was diabolical as soon as we set off, leaving us at a snail's pace on London's Holloway Road. The M6 was a car park. And it was definitely a bad idea to try to cut through part of the urban sprawl of the West Midlands to avoid the motorway jam. And then there was the A55.

When I arrived in Bangor not one of my friends was around. I had been expected at tea-time to pick up some friends for the night out, but it was now about 8.30pm. When I had previously gone to this night club, there were about a dozen of us, but now we were down to two and I had an extra ticket. I was shattered and disappointed to say the least, but the trip had become a challenge, and we carried on, arriving in Liverpool shortly after 11pm and in Cream by about midnight. I had worked the queue until someone bought the spare ticket but then had to meet up with my companion John who had gone 'AWOL'. I was walking up and down, doing my best 'dodgy geezer' impression but found John soon afterwards and made it into the club. We had finally arrived.

Cream consisted of a number of rooms with several bars and a capacity of about 3,000 people. It boasted some of the country's finest DJs, playing the best in contemporary 'garage' and 'hard house'. It enjoyed a friendly atmosphere and little trouble (at least while I was there) in contrast to other clubs such as Manchester's 'Hacienda' where gangland violence, general bad vibes and undesirable goings-on occasionally spilled into the club. When we went to the 'Hac', trouble put a downer on the night and everyone was a bit edgy. At Cream you didn't have to worry about who was watching you – everyone was just there for a good time, and that's what I liked about the place.

It was still a pretty crazy party zone, but the place had changed. Three years is a long time in clubland, with its changing attitudes, fads and fashions, and I am not sure to what extent it was my own perspective that had altered. The euphoric, mad-for-it atmosphere was still better than any of the other clubs though. In 1994, my initial impression of the club had been 'Well what's all the fuss about?' until at about 2am, the place had taken off like a rocket seemingly in a matter of minutes.

The music was good and the vibes even better. I looked through to the next room, only small but with about 150 party people crammed in, dancing like there was no tomorrow. There was full-on cheering, fists punching the air, everyone was having a wild time as their senses went into overload. It sounded mental. Eventually we hit the dance floor, as the pounding beat penetrated our heads then spread through our bodies until every part was moving. We stayed by a group of lads at the edge of the dance floor. They looked the sort to go out on the 'rob' on a typical Friday night but who were now at Cream, part of the feel-good factor and having a great time. They seemed a little in awe of John, a big black guy, shuffling around the dance floor in denim jacket, baseball cap and a 'don't mess with me' scowl. John was a work colleague from Hackney Town Hall. He looked every inch the streetwise urban lad he was. He had not been out of London for about two years and, as I watched him dance, I realised we were worlds apart – my inhibitions were down, but John was too image-conscious to drop the scowl and relax. I was at ease here, even though another part of my world was still hundreds of kilometres away off the Cornish coast, demanding my presence. That night, clubbers were heading from all over the north of England to Cream. And birders from all over the country were heading to 'Scilly'.

The club was rocking now, and screams of delight continued to emanate from parts of the club as the DJ brought the crowd to a crescendo before the break kicked in and the beat exploded back out with a vengeance. The club's Phazon sound system was one of the loudest in the country, and the sound was high quality digital – bass which made your chest vibrate violently and shook the very building we were all in, and amazingly crystal clear treble which cut through your soul with unstoppable force. The club was a seething mass of strobe-illuminated bobbing heads amongst the dry ice-produced 'smoke'. We had gone into autopilot, unable to stop dancing as our body rhythms seemed to tune into the beat which controlled our every movement. Jaydee's epic *Plastic dreams* belted out across the dance floors, turning on a few smiles before the rooms darkened slightly, and everyone danced away their troubles to the throbbing, all-powerful beat. Everyone there felt as one. We were all here with the same purpose – to dance. Time became less meaningful as the hours blurred together, and heads and bodies rocked, unable to stop moving. The music seemed alive and dancing felt good – the only way to release the bottled up energy crammed into each body in the club. Even so, the night was drawing inexorably to its close. The crowd still cheered, the whole club still danced, but it was a world I was about to leave. I had to be in Penzance by 2.30pm to catch the 'chopper' to Scilly, and it was now nearing 6am. The DJs would soon be playing their final set. I had been dancing for nearly six hours without a break and now I had to hit the road without time for a rest. We left the club and returned to the car. I headed south.

John was quiet. Not knowing quite how to explain my predicament, I tried to keep secret my destination but, in the end, had to tell him the truth on the way and explain why I wasn't driving back to London, a fact he had at least been aware of in advance. I told him I had to get to Cornwall to catch a helicopter to the Isles of Scilly as there was a rare bird from America out there I very much wished to see. John did not know I was a birder. He didn't really know what a birder was and refused point blank to believe me. I think he was just about aware that birds existed, had probably never thought about them and seemed incapable of understanding that any of his friends might actually be remotely interested in them. He thought I had been winding him up, but it now dawned on him that I might actually be serious. Certainly, it had been too much for him to take in initially and he was still looking at me as if I were mad, then began to realise that there must be at least some truth in my confession. I dropped him off in Birmingham at the train station and once again set off south.

It was a grey and miserable morning, and it soon started to rain heavily. Visibility was bad, and I began to think that I shouldn't really be driving. I had a rest at several service stations en route and reflected on the night before. I could almost hear the music still. Faces flashed through my mind, and a thousand thoughts. My college days had been a whirlwind of excitement and partying, and a night out clubbing had brought back many memories. There was still a passion for house music within me. For a while, I was once again lost in clubland, thinking about past nights out, reminiscing. But then I was on the M5 somewhere near Bristol and realised that I still had a long way to go.

According to my faithful pager, there was a Sabine's Gull on the Hayle Estuary, West Cornwall, which I really wanted to see. It soon flew off but was relocated on the heliport at Penzance – even more convenient. I put my foot down a little but, unfortunately, the gull didn't stay around long enough for me to see it. I arrived at the heliport in plenty of time and boarded the helicopter, my first trip aboard a chopper. As the large machine's engines burst into life, my ears were subjected to yet another battering as we headed west, out over the fields and the villages and the spectacular rugged Cornish coast below.

The news on the Isles of Scilly was not good. The Common Yellowthroat, earlier observed in a grass meadow near Lower Moors, had not been seen for quite a while, not since the previous day in fact. I had just missed a Corncrake in the same field and contented myself by studying some bush crickets – Long-winged Cone-heads (*Conocephalus discolor*) – that had aroused the interest of a few birders. I waited until dusk. Still no Yellowthroat.

With any other bird, I, and probably most others too, would have given up. However, yellowthroats are notoriously elusive, and there were plenty of people still around checking the area near Rose Hill. I never strayed far, refusing to believe the bird had departed. Then, at last, came the news I had been waiting for. The Yellowthroat had been relocated. I ran like the very wind that had brought it here.

It had moved from Lower Moors further up Porthloo Lane and was reported several times, as huge numbers of people lined up along the lane. But I just couldn't get onto it. Maybe there were too many strobes, roboscans and UV tubes at Cream; whatever, my reflexes were just not sharp enough and my faculties had not fully returned. I was not sure exactly how many hours I had waited for this bird since landing on the islands, but whilst it was apparently still showing, I hadn't yet seen it. The problem remained that it would only show for a second or two, then would dive into cover to reappear perhaps half an hour later a few metres away. As desperation set in, I headed to the top of the bank where a growing number of birders were looking down at the mass of vegetation from Harry's Walls.

Time dragged on. Then at last it popped up in full view about 40 metres in front of us, a dazzling yellow throat, obvious even with the naked eye (see plate 10). Through the 'scope I had an excellent, if somewhat brief, view of the bird. I waited a while longer but never saw it again. Later in its stay it became somewhat easier to see, but I didn't have the patience to wait for long, although I did spend an hour or so most days at the site. Whilst my views had been brief, they had been good and, after all, I was on the Isles of Scilly and wanted to find my own birds.

Apart from the Blackpoll Warbler, a bird many birders had seen previously anyway, this was the only major rarity on the Isles of Scilly during October 1997, making it fairly disappointing in most birders' eyes. Although the star bird was shy and elusive and therefore difficult to see, it eventually stayed long enough for everyone to see it who wished to – right up until 7th November in fact. It constituted the seventh record for Britain and Ireland and the second for Scilly. I had been unable to twitch the female Yellowthroat on Shetland the previous spring, so this individual was particularly appreciated.

The Isles of Scilly are a popular holiday destination with both birders and non-birders alike, with tourism providing the main source of income for the islands, although their increasing popularity has seen the cost of a holiday there rise steeply. They are such an integral part of the rare bird scene that they really deserve a special introduction here. Of around 150 islands, only five are inhabited, with the largest concentration of residents living in Hugh Town on St Mary's. The warm temperatures and high humidity here create a unique sub-climate that supports a wealth of tropical plant life – palm trees abound and Tresco's Abbey Gardens are a botanist's paradise with some 20,000 plant species from 80 different countries. So, there's no excuse for exotic birds from distant lands not feeling at home if they drop in, and the gardens certainly provide pleasant surroundings to look for birds. There is a great diversity of invertebrate life (including more than one introduced species of stick insect) and the islands are also home to the Lesser White-toothed Shrew (*Crocidura suaveolens* ssp. *cassiteridum*), which occurs nowhere else in the British Isles but for a small population on the Channel Islands.

Despite the impressive track record of these islands in attracting rarities, some of the keener birders prefer not to base themselves here in the autumn in case a bird turns up elsewhere in the UK and they run the risk of missing it – particularly as there is no travel to or from the islands on a Sunday. Myself, I prefer the less crowded Cornish valleys at this time of year. They are well within striking distance of the islands, whilst maintaining the convenience of being on the mainland, should I need to head elsewhere.

Many birders have made the annual pilgrimage to Scilly for decades and have seen some impressive rarities as a result. The pubs at this time are full of bird enthusiasts recounting tales about…well…birding. Guesthouses and hotels are usually full, as are self-catering flats. It is the second holiday season of the year for the islands, and everywhere you look you will see at least one person with binoculars. Occasionally, following news of the discovery of a rare bird, a stampede occurs through the main town of St Mary's, Hugh Town. And it's not just birds that can cause excitement. In 1998, a Monarch butterfly (*Danaus p. plexippus*), having just travelled thousands of miles, presumably from North America, settled on an apple tree in a small front garden in Hugh Town, just metres from where I was eating lunch in the popular Bishop and Wolf pub. Within half an hour, nearly 300 birders had assembled, some having chartered taxis from the other end of the island. A keen lot, we birders.

Yes, silliness abounds on the Isles of Scilly. It is a hive of activity for hundreds of birders and the social scene is great. The evening is a time to reflect on the day's sightings over a few pints and have a laugh at the excessive twitching antics of some. My favourite story from a few years back concerns an announcement on CB radio that a birder had located a Common Nighthawk, roosting on one of the islands. This cryptically coloured bird blends into its surroundings when on the ground and can look like a piece of dead wood.

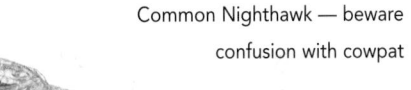

Common Nighthawk — beware confusion with cowpat

It is also an extreme rarity and, at the time, had still not been seen in this country by some of the nation's top birders. Needless to say, panic ensued as frantic arrangements were made to get to the island in question before it decided to fly off. It was only when the 'bird' didn't move however, that the observer noticed something was wrong. It transpired that he was watching some dried faecal matter that somehow, at a particular angle, took on the shape of a Common Nighthawk at rest!

Birders were chartering planes, helicopters and boats, and the national grapevine was buzzing when the birder, who originally made the announcement, was next heard on the CB explaining that he had actually found...a cowpat! Another amusing and well-known incident apparently occurred the year before when play was halted at the Annual Birders *versus* Islanders football match, because the UK's first ever Red-breasted Nuthatch had turned up in Norfolk. That doesn't happen in the football league Premiership.

Back to my story though. A week passed on the Isles of Scilly. The rarities were okay, but other than the two American warblers, there was nothing to write home about. The Chinese Grosbeak was interesting but had come out of a cage somewhere, rather than having flown here from China. So I left on the 18th and stayed the night in the car in a Cornish valley near St Just, hoping to see the reported Rose-coloured Starling the following morning. All I got in the morning, however, was a flat car battery and a visit from the AA. No starling and a worrying dearth of pager messages. I soon found out that I was simply in possibly the worst spot in the UK for receiving messages, and that at least the pager itself was (presumably) still functional. A good old-fashioned call to Birdline was what was needed, and at last my luck began to change. A Radde's Warbler had been spotted just a few kilometres down the road at St Levan.

I left St Levan at around 2.00pm, having enjoyed good views of the warbler and even had had time for a quick sea watch in rather blustery conditions. I was finally on my way back to London, hoping I would miss nothing more on the Isles of Scilly. At around 2.40pm, just as I was heading along the A30 approaching Redruth, a message was broadcast stating there was a report of a Siberian Rubythroat at Osmington Mills in Dorset. If confirmed, this would be just the second for Britain – the only other being a female seen by less than 30 people on Fair Isle in 1975. Needless to say, my foot went down on the accelerator as I attempted another Dorset dash, similar to last year's one when I left the Isles of Scilly prematurely for a Northern Waterthrush at Portland Bill. For a while it was touch-and-go. Was no news good news? Well, negative news certainly wasn't, and when it was revealed the bird hadn't been seen since the initial sighting, I eased off the 'gas'.

At about 4pm, the news everyone interested had been waiting for broke. The Rubythroat had been relocated and was showing well. Faces would have visibly dropped on the Isles of Scilly, but the only thing of mine that dropped was my right foot – once again pressing down on the accelerator. How I wished now that I hadn't slowed down. And how I wished I had a faster car. I was constantly calculating my ETA. I appeared to have enough time as dusk drew closer, but this didn't allow for any delays, more especially if the bird proved elusive or roosted early.

Then disaster struck – I hit traffic near Honiton. Not literally, thankfully, but the practically stationary string of cars, stretching way into the distance, was punishment enough. Something had to be done. I knew if I stayed in this jam it could cost me the bird. Rubythroat is an almost mythical bird that heads many lists of 'most wanted'. I wasn't going to miss one because of a traffic jam if I could possibly help it.

Turning right into a country lane, I looked for an alternative route. These were dangerous roads for someone in my current state of mind, so I reminded myself that if I crashed I wouldn't see the bird – and maybe nothing ever again. Eventually I came back out into the town I had been heading for. Time was fast running out and I began to wonder if I would make it in time. I went all out for it.

As I neared the site, the light appeared to be slowly beginning to fade. Cars had their lights on; I felt like shouting loads of abuse at them, and that it wasn't that dark yet. I raced down the approach road to the mill and parked with the other birders' cars. In such circumstances there is always a dilemma – do you drive to the end to minimise walking/running distance or do you park to save looking for a space? There was no time for thinking about it, and I had to accept that the quickest way to find the spot was to follow birders who had just arrived in the car park. Those arriving at around the same time as me appreciated the seriousness of the situation. Non-birders may laugh but, believe me, this was serious. Everyone was running. No one walked. No one talked.

The light was definitely fading now. We ran down the side of a pub called the Smuggler's Inn and were told by a bemused onlooker where the bird was. Everyone was panicking. As we ran across the field I slowed, cursing my lack of physical fitness, but was reassured by the crowd ahead. I managed a final spurt of energy before, utterly exhausted, I arrived amongst the throng of birders. It was 5.50pm, but the last sighting of the bird had been prior to 5.30pm, I think around half an hour or so before my arrival. Birders were arriving completely out of breath and covered in sweat. Franko, an exceptionally keen London-based birder I knew, had taken charge and decided that everyone should move back, away from the hedge. This was probably a good idea. The minutes ticked on. By 6.00pm people were wondering whether the bird had gone to roost. I refused to believe that this could turn into one of my worst dips ever.

Then suddenly everyone was running. Determined to be first, I sprinted like a gazelle. There was a muddy quagmire by the gate we had to go through, so I slowed enough to keep my balance as I crossed to the next field (I wasn't quite so graceful at this section). Luckily it was just a few metres up the field-edge to view the end of the hawthorn hedge we had been waiting patiently at. Everyone fell silent. Was it a false alarm? I couldn't tell. Then suddenly I heard 'It's just right of the fence post, about 18 inches up'. I peered at the hedge through my 'scope, perhaps unwisely as bins would have found me the bird quicker. The light was gloomy and I panned slowly until...*there it was!* Unmistakable, just sitting there facing us. A small bird with a bright ruby-red throat and short white stripes above and below the eye (the supercilium and moustachial stripe to give them their proper name) (see plate 14). No sooner had I seen it however, than it turned its back on us and disappeared into the hedge. I had wasted valuable seconds getting onto it and had only watched it for a few seconds in, by now, rather gloomy light. It was 6.05pm and more than 300 people had connected with this little gem.

The Rubythroat was never seen again and, to add insult to injury, the 500 or so dippers the following morning got extremely wet. Apparently I was mentioned indirectly in the national press as someone who had made it from the other side of Cornwall (it had taken me three hours). Apart from the odd exception, no one past London or Birmingham made it in time, and it could have been decades before the next mainland individual was seen (although one was actually to appear on Fair Isle in 2003 (see chapter 11) with another in 2005). Sometimes it pays to put your foot down.

Chapter 6

October Thrushes

White's Thrush, *Zoothera dauma*, is a much sought-after Siberian vagrant that had nearly cost me everything (including my home) a few years earlier, yet was perhaps a blessing in disguise. I had returned home from that dip at my lowest ebb. I had initially turned down a trip to see it, then gone days later only to miss the damned thing by an hour and a half, having undergone a gruelling journey to get there. However, in October 1998, I got a second crack at it and joined a long haul trip to the Isle of Lewis in the Western Isles of Scotland, finally to gain revenge on the bird that had 'got away' all those years before. This was personal.

The White's Thrush had been present for some 10 days, so success was likely, or so it seemed. A quick look at the weather though, and potential problems were evident. Heavy rain and gales marked the arrival of an Atlantic front making travelling more dangerous and potentially making it more difficult to look for the bird (although it is bad weather which actually tends to ground these birds in the first place, whilst calm, clear nights often prompt them to continue migrating). Its secretive nature makes flight views the norm and the bird is particularly difficult to see in the field. There is little else of comparable size (a little larger and heavier than a Blackbird, about the same size as a Mistle Thrush) that consistently proves so elusive. As if that was not enough, there was doubt as to whether the boat would actually sail to Stornoway, the main port on Lewis. I didn't feel good about the trip in the slightest, but made my way to Adrian's house in Essex all the same. He had been unable to find out if the boat would sail or not. The whole thing looked rather dubious and we couldn't decide upon going or staying. Eventually we realised we had run out of time. Adrian did the sensible thing. 'If we're going, we'll have to leave now; if we then decide not to, we'll just turn back.'

It seemed like madness. We were unlikely to make the ferry and we didn't know if it would leave anyway. We turned back just before we reached the M1. We had made really good time, covering the distance in about half an hour and, although I had tried to talk Adrian out of going earlier, I was now slightly warming to the idea, my sense of adventure having been roused somewhat by our departure. But our timing was bad. It was Friday night and there were no ferries on Sundays; in fact, the area where the bird was frequenting had no public access on this holy day of the week. It meant that we would have to go across on Monday morning, not even knowing if our bird had been present the previous day! This was an unusual state of affairs and few birders will shift unless they know a bird is definitely still present when they depart. On this occasion though, we had no choice. Once we had turned back, the Monday sailing really was our only option.

The following Monday morning saw four of us sitting in the car at Ullapool, the rain pattering annoyingly on the roof, with the weather still grim. We boarded the large ferry with some two dozen other birders from around the country. We had managed to all club together to get a discount by block-booking the tickets. I found my first Little Auk for ten years (virtually to the day) as it zipped past the boat and, as we neared Stornoway, got onto a buzzard which appeared to have a white tail. It fooled us all for a while but appeared to be a Common Buzzard, rather than the much rarer Rough-legged.

I had never been to the Western Isles before but to be honest there was little to see. Not that I was really concerned with the scenery. We headed north-east in a small fleet of taxis, probably the largest convoy the islands have ever seen. There was some debate as to where the bird was exactly, and the entire fleet had to perform a succession of three-point turns, driving back the way it had come until, at last, the correct spot had been reached.

It really was a barren place, the gardens being much smaller and more sparsely vegetated than we had imagined. There was nowhere for this bird to hide. If it was here, we were unlikely to miss it.

We searched in vain for a long time. It must have been two hours. As far as I, and everyone else present, was concerned (our team now numbered more than 30), we had dipped. We had been in all the gardens (with the residents' permission) yet nothing but the occasional Blackbird had flown out. Buffeted by the wind, I resigned myself to the fact that the mythical thrush had beaten me once again. How could fate be so cruel?

Suddenly, without warning, people started running. There was the usual confusion as everyone struggled to come to terms with what was happening. It could be a false alarm. I managed to secure a lift with a couple I had met previously who had a Ford Fiesta with them, and we travelled the short distance to where the bird had allegedly been sighted. There then followed what seemed like an eternity of what might be termed 'negative news'. We had surrounded a tiny garden. A couple of scouts went in to encourage the bird out, but there was no sign of it. One or two Starlings flew out and then it was quiet. We continued to wait. Eventually it was time for the detective work. Who had seen it? Where? How well? Had only one person claimed to have seen it? Were they sure of the identification? What was their eyesight like? Were they sober? Had they been eating any unusual fungi? Were they clinically sane?

As often happens in these situations, suspicion and pessimism set in as we realised there could be no bird left in this tiny garden... In fact, we were on the brink of giving up when a huge lumbering thrush appeared from nowhere, undulating past the slightly shocked crowd in seemingly dream-like slow motion, underwings blazing black and white glory (see plate 10). White's Thrush had arrived and it certainly knew how to make an entrance! We had travelled a vast distance and thought we had dipped, but at the last minute, the star of the show had made a most spectacular and heart-stopping appearance. The atmosphere was electric. We all grinned and praised each other in awe of the sight we had just seen (see plate 2).

When I have the opportunity of seeing a rare bird, I feel that I witness a natural event that is quite amazing and in certain ways, unique. It is truly a miracle that a bird such as this White's Thrush can journey all the way from China (China no less – just think how far that is; I moan about having to go all the way into town sometimes AND in a car) and be discovered on some far-flung British island. I feel immensely privileged, as if by being there I can be part of it in some way, being part of history in the making. I remember at the age of eight catching a glimpse of the Queen in my home area of East Ham and feeling very lucky – she was the first great rarity I had twitched and although views were relatively brief, I didn't even need my bins. Catching a glimpse of a celebrity is a good comparison to what it's like being in this game. To birders, the birds *are* celebrities. And when it looks like your mission has been unsuccessful, but at the eleventh hour you're proved wrong, it is a great feeling indeed. With the White's Thrush, there was something explosive about its sudden appearance, and that black and white underwing was dazzling. The sight of it flying past me will stay in my memory for ever.

Being October though, the 'high' of seeing a White's Thrush didn't last too long. There was a Hermit Thrush in Ireland and an American Robin on the Isles of Scilly, news of the latter somehow filtering through while we were still combing the gardens of North Tolsta. No sooner had we bagged the White's, than we were planning our next move. In fact, we were all probably planning before we had even seen it, working out if it was actually feasible to see all three thrushes in the space of a few days. We left Ullapool with a plan to head for the Isles of Scilly via Essex where we would collect Adrian's dad. Adrian had carried out all of the driving so far. It had taken ten and a half hours to reach Ullapool from his house and he was now facing the same journey in reverse without sleep. One of the other passengers agreed to drive for a while. It was the only sensible thing to do.

'D'ya know how to drive a rear-wheel drive?' was the only interrogation our new driver received. It seemed not, as within five minutes he had lost control of the vehicle and we had spun off the dual carriageway, ending up in a ditch. Oops. As it bucketed down with rain, we emerged to inspect the damage. It seemed minimal initially but then we noticed that the rear bumper had come off – or so it seemed. However, after a further period of reflection, we realised to our collective amazement that the rear bumper was *apparently* still on the car. In fact, the truth of the situation was more strange: by a quite incredible chance our vehicle had backed onto, with uncanny precision to within a few centimetres, a perfectly fitting bumper that was already in the ditch, presumably the remnant of a previous accident in the same spot! X-Files eat your heart out! We were thoroughly soaked by the time we were pulled out of the ditch by a breakdown truck that took two hours to arrive and, as a consequence of this delay, we were now way behind schedule. There was still a lot of road to cover. At least the Hermit Thrush in Ireland had now gone, so that was one less bird to worry about.

With Adrian back at the wheel, we battled the morning rush hour to pick up his father, Dave, at Grays in Essex and we knew it was touch-and-go if we would make the Isles of Scilly in time. Dave had booked a chopper to the islands from the Cornish mainland just the previous day while we were still on the ferry returning from Uist, but he had paid for it by credit card. Our accident during the night could prove to be more costly than we had anticipated. There was no time to lose. We were at Adrian's house for barely two minutes while we grabbed Dave and his gear.

The weather was still poor as we made for the South-West and Adrian was still driving. He had managed all of the 2000km or so running on adrenalin and caffeine for most of the 40 hours since we had left (about 24 of which had been spent in transit). For our own safety, it was better that Dave took over the wheel. He eventually did so somewhere at a service station along the M4. Visibility was terrible and overtaking became even more treacherous. We were now way behind schedule and our chances of making the chopper flight were fast diminishing. With every calculation of the time we had left, we came to the conclusion 'well we might *just* make it' but also realised that it would be marginal. Pretty soon, the calculations became more pessimistic and it was time to phone the heliport. Adrian assured the staff we were not far away, as we hurtled towards Penzance. Covering the last few kilometres, we realised we would be late and were relying on a bit of sympathy from the heliport staff. The mobile phone was out again. More reassurance. As we drew level with the heliport, the helicopter took to the air. Adrian was on the mobile, trying to bribe the pilot.

'We'll give him forty quid tip, fifty quid, come on,' he pleaded. 'We're just outside!'

But it was to no avail. The helicopter paused in mid-air as we passed, as if the pilot was thinking over the offer, but then it was off, leaving us waving out the window as it thundered overhead. We were now well and truly stranded...or so it seemed.

As luck would have it, we met some friends at the heliport and managed to secure a lift to the Isles of Scilly soon afterwards. The staff had managed to squeeze us on to a later flight but it was going to Tresco, an island from which it would subsequently be difficult to get onto St Agnes, our intended destination; therefore we would have to make our own way to St Mary's. The staff members were torn between bemusement and frustration but were presumably used to such excessive 'twitching' antics as ours at this time of year. I am sure it gives them all a challenge – and laugh perhaps too, but their understanding and co-operation are always greatly appreciated.

When we stepped from the chopper on Tresco, we had a fresh problem. We had to get to either St Mary's or St Agnes. We learnt to our dismay that all the boats to 'Aggie' had been cancelled due to the gale-force winds and that an earlier boatman had been given the run-around by birders wanting to make it across. They had messed up some arrangements or other and he, the boatman, had eventually decided not to take anyone else. Arriving at the quay, we approached a boat and enquired of the boatman standing nearby about transport to St Agnes.

'Not possible. Force seven storm. All boats cancelled,' he said gruffly.

'We'll make it worth your while,' Dave replied with bated breath, and as Adrian flashed some cash around, suddenly those perilous winds were not quite so bad after all. As dusk descended, we chugged out into the raging gale.

The boat was tiny – it could probably have fitted comfortably into my old bedroom – and the waves were certainly big. We sheltered in the front part which was enclosed. Adrian placed his rucksack on the seat but was told it wouldn't remain there for long. He looked at me in a 'What have we let ourselves in for?' sort of way, but only actually said, 'Shit'. It was getting dark outside, and the sea was becoming rougher. Much rougher. The boat rolled violently and we clung on tightly. I should have tried to enjoy the thrilling ride but was too nervous of the boat capsizing. We lurched violently in and out of troughs, constantly losing sight of the horizon a long way beneath the tops of towering, menacing waves which had just rolled in from the Atlantic. I was amazed the sea could be this rough in what I assumed was a relatively sheltered stretch of water. The boatmen – old sea dogs, probably well used to the terrors of the ocean in such conditions – looked rather relaxed, which was a good sign. As we neared the quay on St Agnes, I felt thankful we didn't have to return in such conditions, since it was now dark and the gale was showing no sign of abating. Yet the boatmen had to get back. They would be alright, we hoped.

Now on St Agnes, we made for the only pub around, The Turk's Head, where we ate and had a beer or two. From there we stumbled back to the waiting room in complete blackness, the sort of pitch-darkness city-dwellers never seem to experience. The waiting room lay at the top of the quay; it was the same room I was planning to stay in when I went for the Nighthawk the previous month. It was dirty with dust and cobwebs, had a hard floor and no heating and more spiders than a field guide to the Arachnidae, but it did have a light and even a bench to sleep on. Above all, it had a roof and was actually not too cold, so, fortunately, I slept surprisingly well.

The American Robin was on private land and consequently it was a while before it was found the following morning. Access had been agreed should the bird be re-found. I ambled down to the spot refusing to run, believing that it would not be going anywhere just yet. It was there alright, and the three of us watched it for some time and, as a consequence, were able to leave the island early. As we departed, a boatload of birders arrived from St Mary's, which included a number of familiar faces present at the White's Thrush site on the Outer Hebrides. Few stopped to chat, with the usual anxious expressions that adorn many a face until the bird is actually seen. One such person made the mistake of asking me if it (the robin) was still there and, unable to resist a mischievous urge, I put on my best sympathetic 'Don't-worry-there'll-be-others' face and told him it had just been taken by a Sparrowhawk. Fortunately for them, they scored on the final day of the bird's three-day stay.

This was the first American Robin for nearly 10 years, although incredibly, the 31st for Britain and Ireland (10 of which have been seen in Ireland). As often happens in birding, the species subsequently became much more accessible, turning up on the mainland for many more people to see. Two birds appeared in December 2003: one in Grimsby,

Lincolnshire, (see plates 11 and 16) and one at Godrevy in Cornwall. Both stayed well into 2004, which then went on to produce a record arrival of White's Thrushes in the autumn. Most of these birds were on Shetland, but there were others, including a well-watched bird present for just a day in Easington, East Yorkshire. In 2002, I had to travel just a few hundred metres for one when I learnt that there was an individual on a nearby cliff top on Fair Isle where I was staying at the time. This is strangely ironic after the 3,000 kilometres or so that I had covered trying to connect with my first, but birding is nothing if not unpredictable.

Chapter 7

Cape Clear

I have always been keen to travel to see rarities, but little has ever set me apart from the hordes of other enthusiasts. For a long time, I simply could not compete with the crème de la crème of birding fanatics, whose lives seem to depend on seeing every potentially new bird. They travel alarmingly quickly and miss little. But then a Blue-winged Warbler turned up and I really wanted to see it. Fearing it might only be present for a day, I knew I had to act fast. I realised at this point it was not just a case of how easy it is for one to get away to see it, but also depends on how much 'bottle' one has. Yes, it's a gamble, sometimes not for the faint-hearted. To be honest, I am not particularly good at making tough decisions, but on the 4th October 2000 I had to. After all, if you want the ultimate prizes you must be prepared to spend the cash – and take the risk of wasting it – as some birds, like time and the tide, wait for no man.

This bird was special, however. I suppose I have said that about other birds too, as have many others on various occasions, but this one *really* did seem worth the effort. It is a member of a family of brightly-coloured warblers found throughout North America, wintering mainly in South and Central America. There are several similar families of such birds and they are high on the 'shopping list' of birders visiting North America. Occasionally, certain species turn up here where they are even more sought-after. There can be few birding experiences to match the discovery of one of these little gems. The individuals making it here are often immatures, with some adults in what the Americans call 'fall' (post-breeding) plumage. Though not quite the resplendent jewels they are on their breeding grounds during the spring, they are still pleasing to the eye, and some birds such as this Blue-wing maintain their bright colours. The Blue-winged Warbler's closest relative, the Golden-winged Warbler, with which it frequently hybridizes in its native America, turned up on a Kent housing estate in 1989. Its arrival prompted me, at the tender age of 13, to take part in one of the largest mass-twitches ever, an occasion which required police officers to control the crowd. Like the bird responsible for that occasion, this Blue-wing was the first of its kind to be recorded on this side of the Atlantic. The fact that it had been found so early in the day meant that perhaps for the first time ever, Cape Clear, a small island off the Cork coast where the bird had been found, could be twitched from England on the same day.

I had first visited the Cape at the age of 15 during a birding holiday to southern Ireland. It is one of Ireland's premier rarity hotspots, attracting particularly Trans-Atlantic visitors over the years, as well as birders. The southern tip of the island is an excellent seawatching vantage point, but is not easy to get to. One has to walk across jagged rocks for quite a distance and risk injury if you slip. On a previous trip to Ireland I remember making it to the end with a gashed wrist and broken tripod, the latter jamming between rocks when I stumbled, with one of the legs almost snapping in half. But the rewards were high, and I had enjoyed fantastic views of passing shearwaters and petrels and a huge school of porpoises. Surprisingly perhaps, until 2000, I had never had reasons to twitch the island from England, but this was soon to change.

It must have been around 9.25am when the news broke. There was no messing around with 'possibles' or 'unconfirmed reports' on the message, as often happens when a rarity is first reported. This was the real thing, an undoubted Blue-winged Warbler, a bird which looked like no other. I spent the next couple of hours frantically telephoning birding associates, airlines and airports to arrange a trip. I eventually booked a place on a flight to Cork the following morning out of Stansted Airport, yet I really wanted to be there sooner. A call to Adrian at around lunchtime confirmed there was still a chance to leave today: a place on the 2.15pm flight from Heathrow with him and Steve Webb. I had about two hours. There was no time to think. I had to give it a try, even though I would end up paying for both flights, which ultimately I did. I knew there was a good chance I would be too late, but I jumped straight in the car and stayed in the fast lane of the M25 all the way. Adrian, too, was trying to make it in time, and I spoke to him at least twice on the mobile.

It took me about an hour to get to Heathrow. There was heavy traffic, although luckily no lengthy delays. I now had a new dilemma – parking. I spent about half an hour trying to find the car park and when I did, I was shocked to learn that I would be paying nearly £100 in parking fees alone, as we were not due to return until the weekend and the fees were some £20 per day. I was close to giving up. The plane was due to take off in about half an hour and I was still a long way from the terminal. I had reached the point where nothing would stop me. I parked in the car park anyway and legged it over to the 'Pink Elephant' bus stop. As the bus rolled up, I jumped inside and asked if it would take more than ten minutes to get to the terminal.

'That's pushing it,' said the driver. 'I dunno about ten minutes.'

'Well, could you just –'

'I'll go at the normal speed. I'm not breaking the speed limit to get there,' he interrupted, eyeing me with the sort of expression I normally reserve for Jehova's Witnesses on my doorstep – just before I boot them off. I briefly imagined an ambulance taking him to hospital 'at the normal speed' after I'd decked him. True, looking back, there may indeed have been little he could do to help me but still, what a time to meet a 'jobsworth'.

We trundled along at a snail's pace and the journey must have taken about 10 to 15 minutes in total. Once inside the airport, I looked around frantically. I ran to the Aer Lingus check-in desk that was, to my surprise, still open. The flight was due to depart in 20 minutes.

'Is there still time?' I enquired breathlessly.

'If you run,' answered the checking-in clerk in an annoyingly cheerful manner.

Then disaster struck. I was paying by cheque but had left my cheque guarantee card in the car. By this time, I had convinced myself that the bird would be gone by tomorrow and that I would never get to see one in

Britain or Ireland again. I phoned Adrian. He didn't have his credit card with him and thus Steve was paying for him. I didn't know Steve well but he was my only hope. After a moment of thought I rang Steve.

'Hello, James, you weren't expecting *me* to be on the line were you?' yelled Franko down the phone. The birding scene is full of eccentrics, but there is no bigger character than Franko. I had done a good deal of birding with Franko over the previous couple of years and found him very sensitive to the needs of others, although intense and highly excitable. Generous as ever, he offered to pay for my flight and I was told to run as fast as possible if I wanted to catch the plane.

It was a long way to the departure gate and the journey seemed to take forever. Eventually I arrived and although it was just minutes before the plane was due to take off, boarding was only just beginning as there had been some kind of delay or other. Adrian, Steve and Jan were there along with Franko who was thriving on the stress of the situation and snarling things like 'You're lucky *I'm* here, aren't you?!! You weren't expecting that!! Don't worry about John – you're not *selfish*, you're just *wise*! If you had have phoned *me* first – You...! You...!!' His heightened level of emotion, excitement and rage, left him momentarily beyond words as he tried to think of a suitable insult that could capture his level of disgust with – and contempt for – the idiots which surrounded him. He reminded me of Basil Fawlty at this point.

'I don't see any of the Top Ten here! *Heard* was quoted three-eighty!!!' screamed Franko, leaping about in an agitated state. He was referring to one of the top British listers and the price of an air ticket he had been quoted.

The flight attendants were looking at us with worried expressions, wondering whether to let us on the plane. Everyone was staring at us with our 'scopes, bins, tripods and our various collective expressions bearing a mixture of anxiety, excitement and embarrassment. To make matters worse, we all had pagers and mobile phones going off noisily every few seconds. On boarding, however, things calmed slightly.

Shortly after arrival in Cork, we all lost each other momentarily and cursed Jan for putting his rucksack in with the baggage. We ran into another John, another familiar face who had just arrived on a flight from Birmingham, and went straight to the car hire counter. It was 4.07pm and

Chapter 7

our charter boat was due to depart from Baltimore at 5.30pm. The drive was estimated to take an hour and a half.

In a last minute change of plan, Franko joined John in his car and they followed us. One of Britain's most notoriously fanatical twitchers, Steve, was at the wheel of our car though, and John just couldn't keep up. Steve really was on a mission, and I hadn't gripped a car seat so tightly since being en route to the Slender-billed Curlew in Northumberland two years previously, when my driver had appeared hell-bent on breaking the sound barrier in a knackered Volkswagen Polo (to be fair though, on that occasion, it actually made all the difference). Only one person had seen more birds in Britain than Steve, and it was clear nothing would stop him. The roads were winding and it was raining. Jan and I dropped a few hints to Steve concerning getting us there in one piece, and Steve held back to let the others catch up. We thought we had lost them a while back but suddenly they were behind us again. When Steve realised the petrol tank was nearly empty, we pulled into a garage and watched them pass by. The last stretch was tough, overtaking with a hair's breadth to spare on the narrow roads and gambling with traffic lights. We were cutting it extremely fine and the driving was…well…let's say Steve would have failed his test.

At 5.30pm precisely, we rolled into Baltimore and looked across to the jetty where birders were on board the boat waving and urging us to hurry. Once again, we ran.

By 6.15pm, we were on the island, running up the hill to where the bird was reported to be. It could go to roost at any minute.

By 6.20pm, everyone had arrived safely. Varying amounts of exhaustion were evident according to how fast everyone had run and how fit they were in the first place. The bird was not showing and we waited in silence.

At around 6.25pm, I saw a movement in the hedge which was probably the Blue-winged Warbler, making me possibly the first non-Irish birder to witness the unique event of seeing this species in Europe. Seconds later and it was sitting there for all to see (see plate 11). The atmosphere was electric, not least because the star of the show afforded excellent views and was spectacularly bright, glowing blue, green, yellow and white in the fading light of early evening. Dusk was drawing in, yet eleven of us had made it over to this remotest of islands before many Irish birders would even have known of the warbler's presence. It could easily have departed that night but went on to stay for a week, allowing several hundred admirers, most of whom would have come across the Irish Sea to make the pilgrimage to Clear. Steve was the only Top Ten Lister to make it on the first day; the rest would be here the following day by which time I would be long gone. We Mega-movers 'took no prisoners' that day and unlike our quarry from the good ol' USA, didn't hang around for long.

Plate 1: Crowd waiting to see Europe's first Golden-winged Warbler at Larkfield, Kent (February 1989). Up to 3,000 people visited on this one day alone. Photo by Paul Doherty.

Plate 2: The author on the Lewis Ferry on the way back from seeing the Cinnamon Teal (May 2004). Photo by Elizabeth Noden; The author celebrating after seeing the White's Thrush on Lewis (October 1998). Photo by Adrian Webb.

Plate 3: The rescue on the Scottish west coast; Doomed boat charter – a Swedish tanker stands by while a full-scale coastguard rescue is launched off the coast (November 2000). Photos by Adrian Webb.

Plate 4: Coming in over Fair Isle...and returning – in convoy (October 2003). Photos by author.

Plate 5: Top left, clockwise: The author birdwatching during the Scilly Pelagic; Landing on the beach at Barra; The *Scillonian* in Penzance Harbour (October 2004); Seawatching at Porthgwarra, Cornwall (August 2002). Photos by the author.

Plate 6: The Purple Martin twitch in September 2004. Heading for Lewis in a small chartered aircraft for the elusive bird. Birders visiting later in the day missed it. Photos by author.

Plate 7: Birders at the Masked Shrike twitch, Kilrenny, Fife (October 2004). Photo by author.

Plate 8: Razorbill and Ancient Murrelet (top); Pine Grosbeak – Oil pastel study by the author aged 17, completed shortly after returning from seeing the bird on Shetland.

Plate 9: Gannet and Black-browed Albatross (top); Blue-cheeked Bee-eater.

Plate 10: Common Yellowthroat (top); White's Thrush.

Plate 11: American Robin (top); Blue-winged Warbler.

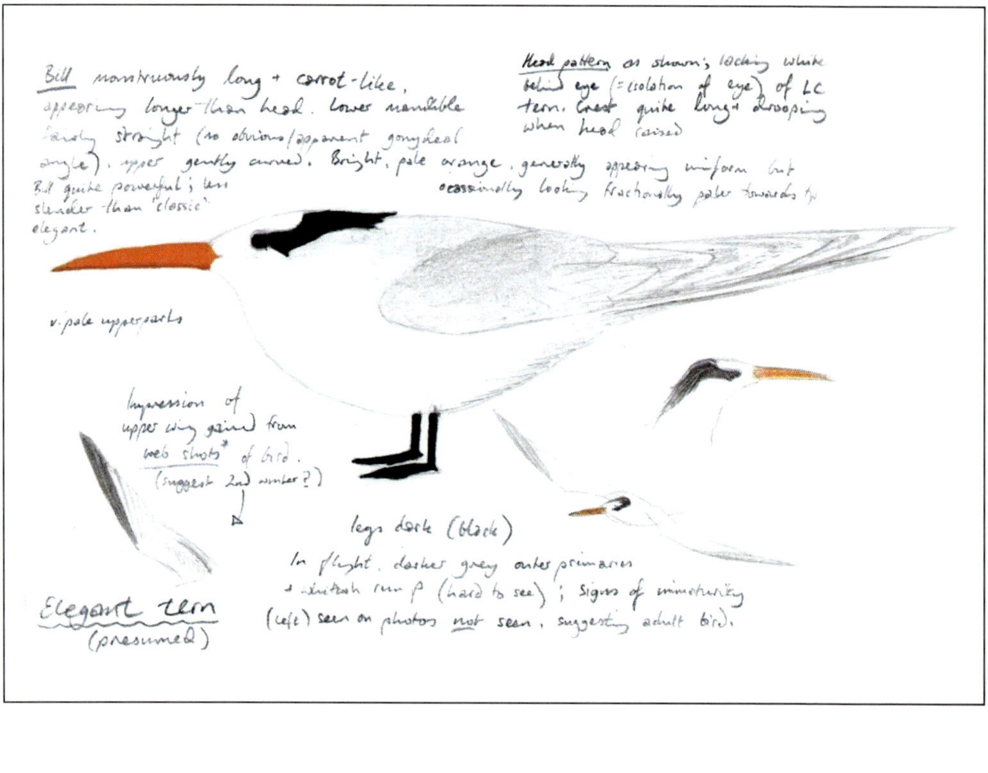

Plate 12: Gray Catbird (top); Elegant Tern.

'mini pelagic' - Scilly light SSE wind
(5 miles S of Scilly)
Great shearwater   7+
Bonxie   1
Storm petrel   numerous
Wilson's petrel   6+ (incl. 3 together +
'Blue' fulmar   1   1 to 5 yrds)

no wing
shape/
less fluttering
flight.

broad pale covert
bar, varying in
intensity, depending
on stage of moult

yellow
webs!
(at 10 yrds range)

more extensive
white rump

slightly squarer-
ended tail than storm
- Projecting feet at close
range

wings often
looked less
swept-back when
compared to storm
petrel.

About 1/3 larger than storm
with longer paddle-shaped wings. Flight gliding, more direct

Plate 13: Wilson's Petrel.

Plate 14: Top left, clockwise: Purple Martin; Siberian Rubythroat – immature female on Fair Isle (October 2003); Siberian Rubythroat – immature male at Osmington Mills, Dorset (October 1997); Savannah Sparrow.

Plate 15: Top left, clockwise: Ovenbird (photo by Adrian Webb); Western Sandpiper; Bullfinch – female of one of the Russian races – on Fair Isle. Slightly greyer than 'our' version with a characteristic nasal call (photo by author); Cream-coloured Courser – Isle of Scilly (September 2004); Yellow Warbler – Barra, Western Isles (October 2004) (photo by Adrian Webb); Masked Shrike – this young bird was the first of its species to be recorded here.

Plate 16: Top left, clockwise: Chestnut-eared Bunting; American Robin – a young male at Grimsby, Lincs. (January 2004), photo by Adrian Webb; Cream-coloured Courser; Belted Kingfisher. Other photos by the author.

Chapter 8

The Rescue

Coming across a shrike whilst birding in Britain or Ireland is always likely to get the pulse racing. Several species occur here on an annual basis but none is common. Sadly, we have recently lost the Red-backed Shrike as a breeding species but it occurs regularly as a migrant (especially at East coast headlands), and the smart-looking Great Grey Shrike is a rare winter visitor. The family name *Laniidae* comes from the Latin *Lanius*, meaning 'butcher'. Yes, these ferocious little songbirds are often called 'butcher birds'. They watch for prey – usually large insects but often lizards, small mammals or other birds – from a prominent vantage point before swooping down on it. Many species rather gruesomely impale their prey on thorns, twigs or other sharp objects, stocking up their larder to feed from at their will. As well as providing a convenient storage facility, this practice may help the shrike hold down its food while it tucks in – the bird lacks the powerful talons of a true bird of prey yet does have a strong hooked bill which comes in useful for killing victims and carrying them off.

The night of the 4th November 2000 saw a number of birders heading to the Isle of Skye to take a ferry to South Uist, Outer Hebrides, when the first ever Long-tailed Shrike for Britain was identified on the island. I first saw this species around the resort of Kuta in Bali in 2000 where it is common, but this didn't make me any less keen to go and see a 'British' one.

The Rescue

Leaving at around 9.00pm, my carload of birders, containing myself and three others, embarked on the 12-hour journey to Uig on the Isle of Skye. It was my second trip to the Western Isles and the third time I had been on Skye. The last was when I had driven from London to see a pair of Northern Bottle-nose Whales (*Hyperoodon ampullatus*) a couple of years before. It is a beautiful part of the country but, as usually happens on these trips, there was insufficient time to explore it and we had had to enjoy the spectacular scenery from the car. We made arrangements to be taken across to Uist on a small fishing boat which would bring us back the same day – to the envy of many others who would be forced to miss work, as the main ferry was not due to return until Monday.

The boat was a little late in arriving and small was not the word. This was a bathtub. I wondered if there were enough paddles to go round. But it was a bright day. The weather was not as bad as had been feared. The bird was still present and to me it seemed to be in the bag, so to speak. There were twelve of us on the boat and we were excited about the prospect of seeing a British first to round off the autumn.

It wasn't long before we were overtaken by the big passenger ferry which rapidly became a disappearing dot on the horizon. We also soon started to get rather wet. Some of us were suitably attired in waterproofs, others were not. Mark was most definitely not, yet curiously insisted on standing where he was likely to get the most spray. He is obviously someone who likes to suffer for his art. We held on tightly as the boat rolled and swayed violently.

After an hour and a half of such gyrations, we were only about halfway across when an unexpected problem arose. The engine conked out and we were suddenly stranded in the middle of nowhere. Apparently, the gearbox had broken. We drifted helplessly for two and a half hours. Attempts to repair the gearbox failed, and I believe that we were seemingly out of range to use the boat's onboard radio to call for help. I was wondering if there was a marine equivalent of the AA when it gradually began to dawn on me that this was potentially a rather serious situation we were in. We were stuck in a tiny boat halfway to the Hebrides, with a storm forecast to hit the Scottish west coast perhaps within the next 24 hours. We had to face the reality of the situation that we found ourselves in and hence, that we might not make it to Uist that day. But the incident had more sinister

Chapter 8

implications: it might actually mean missing the bird altogether.

Soon two of the passengers were being sick over the side. Anxiety swept through the boat. Some did manage to remain cheerful, chatting and laughing, but others just looked depressed. Johnny hung his head and jammed his fists into his jacket pockets, appearing to enter a state of torpor from which he emerged briefly to explain he was conserving energy. By now my feet were soaked from the water swirling round the deck. They had been for some time and I was finding it difficult to move my toes.

For what seemed like an eternity, no one knew what was happening. Matthew was on the phone over-dramatizing the situation. He was using phrases such as 'If I don't see you again' and 'If we get out of this alive…' much to everyone's amusement, although in truth, looking back on the incident, he could have been right!

Then we heard the lifeboat was on its way along with a coastguard helicopter. A Swedish tanker appeared to be heading straight for us. It pulled to a halt nearby, seeming to do an oil tanker equivalent of a handbrake turn, and remained on standby (see plate 3). The helicopter arrived and circled above us for half an hour or so. We had a rather stilted conversation with the occupants of the tanker, stilted partly because only one side had a loud hailer and partly because they spoke mainly Swedish, but even so, kindly managed to communicate to us the fact that the lifeboat was on its way. The tanker then turned again and began to move off. The lifeboat was now approaching and we waved a goodbye to our Scandinavian friends.

It took another hour and a half to be towed back to the Isle of Skye. News of the air-sea rescue had already reached birders at the Shrike site, and I had a phone call from Franko who yelled at me down the phone to arrange another charter. He had been trying to do this, but all I desperately wanted now was a change of dry socks. The police were waiting for us on the quay and took all our names and addresses. When they heard about what we birders had been up to and our dice with death on the high seas, they at least left with something to laugh about with their colleagues down the pub that night!

There was more confusion as everyone decided what to do next. A miniature influx of rarities had hit the UK and more than half of the crew needed at least one of the two rare American thrushes which had just turned up further south. One carload headed to Cornwall for an American Robin, about a 14-hour drive, with another group intending to do the same but then come straight back for the next crossing to Uist the following day! I just wanted to get home, which thankfully was where my driver was heading. The second carload apparently changed their minds about Cornwall and did subsequently get across for the Shrike...after it had gone. Looking back, there was one question that bothered me on that boat and which may well have crossed the crew's minds during the ordeal…why didn't I just stick to stamp-collecting?

Chapter 9

The Siege

Any bird turning up on the British mainland, which has never before been seen by the birding community, can expect a lot of attention and at least several hundred visitors. Even those on offshore islands occasionally draw such numbers and, if a rarity hangs around for more than a few days, then thousands may come to see it. In the competitive world of twitching, many individuals think of certain sightings in the same way as an antique collector looks on his most prized piece. There are always short-staying birds which are seen by relatively few people and, for those individuals concerned, it can be a very privileged feeling to have been one of the 'lucky few'. Many birders are often torn between wanting their friends and other birders to connect with a bird which has just given them much pleasure, and wanting the little blighter to disappear, thus making them feel all the more lucky for having witnessed such an exclusive sighting. Of course, few openly admit to this, but some have confided to me that this is the case and I reluctantly admit that I know how they feel. I genuinely want most birds to be accessible to everyone and I enjoy watching others getting a kick out of seeing a bird. But when you take the trouble (and expense) to get to a bird quickly, it can be frustrating when that bird goes on to stay for a month. It can cost hundreds of pounds to reach an offshore island the same day, but there is often a cheaper alternative if you're not in a hurry. So it's nice to have a few exclusive sightings as a reward for your dedication. That said, most birders (myself included) tend to help others as much as they can to see a bird by quickly relaying any news of its initial presence or continued whereabouts. So it is altruism that wins over elitism in the end.

When a Gray Catbird turned up near Holyhead mid-week during October 2001, it was exceptionally difficult to see and consequently only around 70 people saw it during its two-day stay. The first for mainland Britain, it followed sightings in Jersey in 1975 and Ireland in 1986. More recently one had hitched a lift on board the liner the *SS Queen Elizabeth II*, and was still on deck when it arrived in Southampton. Clearly, the prospect of a holiday in Southampton Docks didn't appeal and it refused to leave the ship, being carried off to another far-flung destination when the vessel left. Rumour has it, it didn't even have a ticket.

Back to the story though. I had taken two weeks off work and it was on the 4th October that my plan looked as though it was to pay dividends. When news of the catbird broke, with nothing to keep me in London, I swiftly packed a bag and left on my now annual jaunt to the South-West via the usual route of everywhere that's not really on the way to the South-West. On this day the previous year (2000), I had flown to Cork for the Blue-winged Warbler and, like that bird, the catbird was to be the highlight of the birding month.

The journey to Anglesey was largely uneventful…until that is I was nearly killed minutes before entering the port of Holyhead. I was travelling in the outside lane of the A5 on an open road when a kamikaze motorist decided to pull out round a particularly slow-moving truck right in front of me. I was way too close to brake so held the accelerator to the floor whilst at the same time alerting (in no uncertain terms) my presence to this crazed idiot. The offender, incredibly, did not take evasive action but continued to come out, forcing me onto the central reservation. I squeezed through with a hair's breadth to spare, gesticulating wildly. Luckily I never laid hands on the other motorist: it would not have been a pretty sight.

Upon my arrival, news broke of a 'vireo species' at the same site. But things were all going awry! I missed this bird by seconds, thanks to a fellow observer's inability to communicate that he was watching it a couple of metres from where I stood, but I relaxed when I heard it was a Red-eyed Vireo and nothing rarer. Any other vireo could constitute another 'first' or perhaps a 'second' record for Britain. After 45 minutes there was no further sign of it, so I pressed on toward the 'catbird crowd'.

It was a dispiriting sight to behold. An army of five-legged soldiers (every birder carries a 'scope on a tripod) formed a battle-line from which they glared at the 'enemy' – a clump of gorse bushes. These bushes may have attracted the bird in the first place but now they stood between us and the star of the show. And the star had a serious case of stage fright. Perhaps there would be no show today. It started to rain. Richard Millington once described the atmosphere at a crowd on the Isles of Scilly who were waiting for a no-show Hermit Thrush as 'resembling Wimbledon's Centre Court after someone had stolen the ball'. Well, this was the same. Only here rain had stopped play. Between this and the wind, there was little chance that our quarry would show itself.

Two hundred people buried their heads in their hoods and wished they had never become birders. After some four hours, darkness fell and so I set off to find my 'luxury accommodation', which eventually turned out to be the Nissan Micra I had arrived in. It wouldn't quite get the full five stars but it kept me dry for a night and even allowed me some sleep.

Dawn saw a resurgence of troops back to surround the thick gorse compound the catbird had last been seen flying into. There were only perhaps 70 or 80 people present. By mid-morning, it was a full 24 hours since the bird had been seen but we would not be deterred. The stand-off continued. This was a siege.

Then, sometime around lunchtime, two birders were standing inside the compound when they saw it. The troops pressed forward in a mad dash. Previously assumed to be impenetrable, the head-high spiky gorse now became a challenge, a kind of assault course as a few brave souls with little regard for their own personal discomfort attempted to flatten some paths through it. It worked. About half an hour later I was standing on the edge of a group of people at the start of one of the newly created 'pathways', wondering how anything could possibly be so elusive as this particular bird. Then suddenly, as if by magic, a long-tailed dark grey bird with a black cap flicked across and perched briefly on the bracken barely three metres in front of me, before disappearing into the depths of the gorse – it was the Catbird (see plate 12) and a moment I will never forget. At that time, less than a dozen people had observed this species in the UK and I was one of the lucky ones. I was over the moon.

Unfortunately, the feel-good factor was dampened almost immediately when I realized I had lost my mobile phone. By the time it turned up some while later, the bird had been showing again. The group further up on the hill were treated to views when it appeared along the field edge. Needless to say, there was much panic and frantic running around as birders tried to anticipate where it would show next. By far the most amusing sight was that of Anthony (a fanatically keen Midlands birder, known to some of his friends as 'Turtle') attempting to cross from the compound to the field. I can still see in my mind's eye in slow motion what happened next: like some demented English collie during the opening credits of 'Lassie', he gracefully leapt over the wall, diving head first into the thick brambles growing alongside it. Shaking himself free of the thorny tangles he had landed amongst, he sprinted across the field. Nothing would stop this man from getting his bird!

The small crowd in the compound, of which I was a part, had been having a hard time. Soon afterwards, however, the Catbird appeared on the wall in front of us and cocked its tail. In a flash it was gone and no one could quite believe what they had just seen. Smiles erupted and backs were slapped. There was even some clapping and cheering. At least three quarters of those present had seen it but they couldn't have numbered more than about 70 people at most. About half a dozen people – mainly RSPB staff – had seen it just after its discovery the previous morning. I had seen the bird after a ten-hour wait, or 22 hours if you count the time spent sleeping in the car. I left 24 hours after my arrival. There were one or two more sightings after I had left, but the Saturday crowd the following day were to be disappointed, although there were a number of dubious claims of birds mainly seen in flight (the question of whether the bird was still present on this day is still debated).

I feel sorry for those that missed the bird on its first day and who had to return to work the following day. I hope that they eventually get another chance to see a 'British' Gray Catbird. When I think of the most memorable moments I have had during my birding 'career', the one when I first saw the catbird will always stand out as a highlight – because, in that moment, despite the fact that it had never turned up in Britain before and that practically no one had yet connected with it, it was just me and the bird exchanging eye contact. And that was just a bit special.

Chapter 10

Day Trip to Dingle

For some years now, I have found myself travelling the length and breadth of the British Isles in search of rare birds. A rather obsessive hobby for sure, with long journeys frequently undertaken at very short notice. One of the pleasures of this is of course the journeying itself and the opportunity to visit little known corners of both Britain and Ireland. Any excuse to visit Ireland is seized upon, as not only is it the homeland of some of my ancestors, but it is also a good excuse to catch up with the family and drink vast quantities of alcohol. Unfortunately, finding time for these pleasures on a collective birding trip is not always possible when the schedule is tight, but it's nice on the occasions I get to travel on my own and with time to spare.

In October 2002, a 'possible' Elegant Tern was reported in County Kerry. Identification of this species, part of the 'Orange-billed Tern' complex, is far from straightforward, and opinion on the Irish bird was divided. I knew that a hop across the Irish Sea was looming however, after studying a series of photographs of the bird on the web. I was convinced that it was an 'Elegant' from the evidence in front of me. My undoubted 'bogey-bird' for most of 2002, it gave many in the birding community the run around, being seen for just single days at Dawlish in south Devon and was apparently never present the following day. Although turning up at a weekend, I initially declined a trip to see this one, for as with the Irish bird that followed, it was first identified as a Lesser-crested Tern – a bird I had seen in Norfolk more than ten years earlier. When the mistake was realised, there had been precious little daylight left, and the following day it was gone. Some weeks later, however, it returned and once again I made the pilgrimage the next day only to find myself stood up yet again. Its reappearance in Wales came at a bad time for me, and when it left there, I really thought I wouldn't get another chance, at least for some while, possibly years.

There followed some confusion as to the identification of the species, with individuals turning up in Holland and Norfolk furrowing even the experts' brows. One of the problems it seems was the existence of hybrid birds as a result of the tendency of Lesser-crested and Elegant Terns to interbreed with local Sandwich Terns. Careful observation of a whole suite of plumage characteristics, not to mention structure and moult strategy, would be necessary to clinch the correct identification of suspect individuals. As a result, there were a number of records of unidentified 'Orange-billed' terns around the country that summer, but on the photographic evidence, I was sure that the Irish tern was an Elegant. Even if it wasn't, seeing it would be an educational experience, and worth the trip.

I had spent two days trying to organize a trip to see this particular bird in Ireland and eventually found a couple of fellow birders – Paul Holmes and Adrian Riley – heading over for it by car and ferry. It was a gruelling journey. Five hours either side of the Irish Sea plus a four-hour crossing in force 5-7 gales. The fine weather we had in Wexford in the morning soon gave way to cloud and stronger winds. And rain – lots of it. If Ireland could export its precipitation, it would be the new superpower. After what seemed a never-ending journey, we arrived at the west coast resort of Dingle with a severely abused suspension system and just over an hour to spare before we had to head back in order to catch the ferry. That meant 30 hours travelling just for one hour's birding! The car seemed to have a pothole-location device set to maximum interception. I had forgotten how bad some Irish country roads can be. On our arrival at Dingle, the weather was still foul and we split up to look for the bird. I had been to Dingle once before, about 12 years previously, to see the famous dolphin 'Funghi'. Funghi has done more for the region's tourism industry than Guinness has for the whole of Ireland, with flotillas of small boats taking droves of tourists out into the bay on a daily basis to meet the charismatic cetacean against the attractive backdrop of the Dingle Peninsula.

There was no time today to look for the dolphin however…if it was still there. We scanned the surrounding shoreline carefully and, amazingly, within ten minutes, located the Elegant Tern sitting on mud some way off. Adrian did a little dance of joy then ran off to find Paul while I watched it from the comfort of the car. The most striking feature of our quarry was the monstrously long, carrot-like bill (see plate 12). It was fairly powerful, seemingly lacking the slender appearance of that of a 'classic' Elegant's bill. It also lacked the reddish base suggested by some of the web photos but did sometimes appear slightly paler and yellowish toward the tip. Lastly, it sported the 'ageing hippy' head pattern typical of the species in winter (where the black on the head is likened to a receding hair-line – I just love that) and lacked any white immediately behind the eye.

When we had had our fill of viewing it, we left Dingle and its graceful bird and headed for Wexford through the wind and rain, and those little Irish towns consisting almost exclusively of pubs and churches. As my uncle, a born and bred Kerry man, once explained, there is a culture in the area of drinking for half the weekend, then spending the remainder of it saying sorry. I am sure he was on the way back from the pub not the church at the time of this remark.

Despite the continuing inclement weather, including gale force winds and driving rain, it appeared that the ferry company would attempt to sail on schedule and thereby make up for any time previously lost…which is more than could be said for us. We were way behind schedule and dashing to catch the boat. On the final stretch, we were nicked for speeding by the police and fined 60 Euros before arriving too late: the boat was still there but the bow doors had been shut early. The following morning's sailing was cancelled, as were all Irish Sea crossings from other locations due to the stormy conditions. Two of us needed to be back at work in England on the Monday, so this was a far from ideal situation. We did the only thing we could in the circumstances; we hit the nearest pub and stayed there until 1.00am.

I awoke at about 6 o'clock in the car, to the sound of Paul snoring, alleviated to some degree by a kick from my size ten boot through the back of the seat. We had an early start, setting off for breakfast in a local café. We amused ourselves by examining the checklist of motoring offences on the back of the speeding ticket and realizing that Adrian had managed to commit the majority of these in the space of our 24 hours in the country, to the would-be tune of several hundred, or perhaps even several thousand, Euros. After breakfast we headed through the town centre to the nearby Garda station to pay the fine (driving without a seatbelt – 19 Euros) whereupon Ade exacerbated our woes by driving the wrong way up a one-way street (60 Euros) and nearly running over a dog (not listed but surely punishable by deportation if only the ferries had been sailing). A trip to the bank furnished us with some local currency for food and motoring offence fines. Until then we had paid the various young shop assistants in sterling where we could, with reactions which ranged from fleecing us on a 1:1 exchange to asking us what the exchange rate was and guessing the amount of change, to taking whatever bank note we gave them and refusing to give any change so as not to confuse the situation further.

We soon headed for Wexford North Slob (truly called this), Ireland's premier wildfowl reserve, covering some 550 acres, and which is located at the western end of the 2,400 acres of 'polder land' claimed in 1847 from the sea. Here we had good views of a 'Ringtail' Hen Harrier and less good views of a distant Peregrine, sitting – unusually – in a ploughed field. The Snow Goose, apparently present in the area, failed to materialise amongst the Greenland White-fronted Geese seen, but we did observe three Irish Hares (*Lepus timidus hibernicus*), currently classed as a subspecies of the Mountain Hare (*L. timidus*) found in Scotland. From here, we travelled to Carnsore Point where late migrants were in evidence in the form of a Swallow, a Wheatear and at least 30 Sandwich Terns offshore, along with two summer-plumaged Great Northern Divers which flew west. By now, daylight was limited and, within a few hours, we found ourselves finally boarding the ferry homeward bound.

It was nice to be able to use toilets on board which didn't resemble a hospital ward during an epidemic of food poisoning – as they had on the way over when I had felt very much like a tennis ball in a match between port and starboard – and we wasted little time in locating the bar. We soon lapsed into a heavy discussion on species concepts but the intellectual debate was short-lived as lack of sleep suffused with some good beer quickly began to take over. The three scientists were thus replaced by three dishevelled and exhausted birders who had not changed their socks since Friday last. It was time to get our heads down for a few hours rest. I was due in work at 9.00am the next day. 'Some nice-looking women on this boat…' was one of the last comments I remembered.

Fair Isle's Double

Halfway between the Shetlands and Orkneys lies a small undulating island, famed for its knitwear – and its birds. Named Fridarey ('Island of Peace') by Norse settlers, Fair Isle, like the Shetlands themselves, is steeped in cultural heritage and wildlife. There are archaeological remains dating back 5,000 years, and historic shipwrecks litter the treacherous coastal waters here. Just five kilometres long and three wide at its broadest point, the north and west of the island is wild and windswept with towering cliffs and a few sheltered 'geos' and burns. The south of the island is flatter and this is where traditional crofts provide a rich diversity of flowers as well as further shelter for many migrating birds in narrow ditches and amongst small plantations of crops.

Fair Isle has long attracted birders from all over the country eager to cash in on the incredible magnetic attraction the island has to wandering birds that come from all directions, but especially from the east. In September, there can be falls of thousands of common migrants such as warblers and thrushes in suitable weather conditions, particularly when easterly winds dominate, and major rarities can turn up on a daily basis. Certain species, such as the Pechora Pipit and Lanceolated Warbler, which hardly ever turn up anywhere else in Britain, seem to be annual on the island. In fact, Fair Isle turns up more rare birds than any other similar-sized location in Britain. For the rarity-hunter it is a veritable paradise. Finding rare birds yourself is never easy, and to be in with a good chance you have to be out all day, every day and in all weathers. On Fair Isle, the birds arrive exhausted and the dearth of vegetative cover means that normally shy and skulking species can be seen hopping about in the open. It is for this reason, coupled with a blanket observer coverage, that relatively few birds go undetected when they arrive there.

I first visited the island in the spring of 1998 and, although I stayed just two days, I came away with an impressive list of birds, including Red-throated Pipit, Bluethroat, Common Crane, Dotterel, and several Red-backed Shrikes. I returned for a week in September 2002, having worked out that this would give me my best chance of seeing a Pechora Pipit in Britain. I wasn't disappointed. Incredibly, three were present on the island the day before my arrival and one was still loitering amidst the crofts, as I sprinted there from the airstrip the following day. I seem to remember it took some finding and when I did finally locate it, I was so awe-struck that I foolishly yelled to the other birders who were also looking and scared the bird off in the process. (I made a mental note of the first birding commandment: 'Thou shalt stay cool, calm and collected when faced with a rarity and not scream like a banshee to attract attention.' I really should have known better on that one). However, the Pechora party wasn't over yet and as I made my way to the airstrip a week later for my departure flight, news of another sent me once again sprinting to the south of the island. I got it by the skin of my teeth.

A year later, the 18th October 2003 dawned cold and grey on an airfield in the north of England, with winter thrushes newly arrived in good numbers and a Tawny Owl showing itself briefly at first light. Somewhere out of sight, a Brambling betrayed its presence with its nasal call. I was with three other birders waiting for a small plane we had hired for the day to get us to Fair Isle for the 'double whammy' of Savannah Sparrow and Siberian Rubythroat, both of which had only been recorded twice previously in a live state on British soil (there was another Rubythroat which was found dead). That both had already occurred on Fair Isle before bears testimony to the island's reputation as a rarity magnet. We spent the first couple of hours engaged in the frustrating pastime of 'waiting on news'. Then there came the news I had been dreading. Not, for a change, that one or both the birds were gone, rather that the Rubythroat was still there. Why a problem? Because it meant we would now go, rather than wait for the news of the Sparrow. I had seen Siberian Rubythroat in the UK already – it was one of the most memorable birds on my British list and had been seen by few of my contemporaries. As much as I would like to see another, I did not relish the thought of spending around £300 for the privilege. During the night, I had been running through my mind the possibility and I now had to make a decision. After some hasty discussions with my 'crew', it was agreed that I would go, but if the Sparrow was gone, I would only pay half. This was fair as the original plan (at the time of the arrangements and before the Rubythroat turned up) was to wait on news of the Sparrow.

It must have been at least half an hour later that news of the Sparrow came through and I breathed a sigh of relief from my seat next to the pilot, a few thousand metres above the English countryside. The moment was marked by much celebration behind me, until one of the complement realised there was nowhere on board to empty his bladder. We looked round for a hole in the plane but the poor chap eventually had to make do with a bottle passed to him. I made a mental note of what the bottle of orange juice looked like, in case I fancied a swig later. It doesn't bear thinking about, really.

I stared blankly at the controls in front of me, wondering what the pedals at my feet were for.

'Why are there two steering wheels?' I naively enquired of the pilot, unaware of the correct terminology for the metal column just in front of me, nor the reason for their duplication.

'If I have a heart attack,' he replied casually, 'you'll have to fly the plane'.

'Oh, right, silly me,' I replied somewhat nervously.

I had been promoted to reserve co-pilot on account of my extensive flying experience, which consisted of being a passenger many times, and once even sitting next to the pilot (as I was now doing) on a Skybus trip to the Isles of Scilly. I was also fully trained in the art of emergency evacuation of an aircraft, having once jumped out of a plane at around 4,000 metres over Lake Taupo in New Zealand, so I was clearly up to flying a plane in an emergency. Anyway, it was exhilarating to be in this tiny six-seater en route to Fair Isle. After two hours and 45 minutes, we descended through some rather poor weather – thick cloud with drizzly rain – with the airstrip on Fair Isle in our sights (see plate 4). The pilot swung us in tightly, straightening up at the last minute, as we jolted down onto the runway in a far from textbook landing. We had arrived.

We were whisked off in the observatory white van down to the two birds. The van famously flies a red flag when a rarity is discovered on the island. During migration seasons, Fair Isle is well covered by birders and this tends to be the best way to put the news out. Everybody looks for the flag whenever the van is about, and on my last visit it had sent me half-running, half-limping down Ward Hill, the island's highest point, where an Alpine Swift had been discovered. I had an in-growing toenail that had turned nasty (and could be approached only with extreme caution). I was wearing the only footwear I could fit my poor swollen and bandaged foot into – a pair of wellies two sizes too big. Every few paces my foot slipped and I yelped in pain, but it was okay – I saw the swift. In fact, I had on several previous occasions been in the said van when pursuing other major rare birds, and had also at other times when on foot (oh happy days!) dived out of its way, as warden Deryk Shaw behind the wheel proved that 'white van man' is alive and well, even on Fair Isle. He took few prisoners when and if his passengers were en route to see a good bird…unless, of course, those on the road had not seen it either, whereupon they might be offered a lift rather than run over.

I reflected on how different the habits of the two birds were. The Savannah Sparrow had been virtually glued to the spot since it arrived, frequenting a feeding station and gorging itself on grain. The Siberian Rubythroat on the other hand, was mobile and elusive and it took a lot of searching to locate it. After giving us all the run around, it finally surrendered by hopping about on the ground beneath the stone walls, when 30 or so twitchers connected with what may well have been their most wanted British bird. For me, the Sparrow was the biggest prize, but on this day, the real star of the show was undoubtedly the Rubythroat (see plate 14). In fact, several observers had travelled up twice to get both of these, some even making it from the Isles of Scilly.

The Sparrow was showing at a distance of just seven metres, an unmissable as well as unforgettable opportunity to study this Trans-

Atlantic vagrant (see plate 14). It happily dined with the larger House Sparrows and Greenfinches, all of which seemed totally unconcerned by the procession of admirers at such close quarters. On one occasion, it showed well for about five minutes before flying out of sight, but we returned later and it was feeding in the same spot yet again. By this time, both birds were 'under the belt' and we were ready to return home. A steady stream of small aircraft had been arriving from all over the north of England and Scotland throughout the morning and the normally empty airfield was now looking decidedly busier with half a dozen aircraft present. We left the island feeling contented but tired and were deposited at Wick Airport for a couple of hours while the pilot kindly flew back to the island to rescue a party of birders whose plane had broken down.

By mid-evening, we were again homeward-bound in a three-plane convoy (see plate 4). Somewhere over the north of Scotland, some friends of ours overtook us, passing by within tens of metres of our wingtip, waving vigorously from their smaller and quicker four-seater. We followed them south and I shut my eyes, smiling both with contentment and at the lunacy of it all.

Chapter 12

All At Sea

For a single memorable day out, it is hard to beat a 'pelagic', a birding trip on a boat which takes you far out to sea to search for ocean-going seabirds. One of the most significant events on the birding calendar, the *Scillonian* pelagic trip out of Penzance, offers the chance of seeing the once 'mythical' Wilson's Petrel. It was mythical to a degree in the days of my first pelagic back in 1989. This was some three years after seabird expert Peter Harrison's discovery of small numbers of this bird in the 'Wilson's Triangle', an area of open ocean more than 100km off the Cornish coast in the western approaches, although even then sightings were regular. After the initial excitement, however, there followed a few lean years when the species was often elusive, and I think the *Scillonian* pelagics even stopped for a while. Thereafter, sightings of Wilson's soon became annual, with the *Scillonian's* success rate of connecting with the species significantly improved, perhaps as a result of a better understanding of where the birds were.

A pelagic is quite a day out. Leaving Penzance quay at around 5.00am (see plate 5), the boat steamed out into the Atlantic, past the Isles of Scilly and into the unknown (well, relatively speaking...). We braved a gale force 6 back in 1992, the year I skipped the trip aboard the *Scillonian* and went in a small catamaran, but the weather was more pleasant on this outbound journey. Nevertheless, I have yet to witness an afternoon out here which could not be described as 'pleasant'. With the trips usually being held in August, fine sunny weather always seems to set in eventually.

On this particular trip I slept for the first hour or so. When I awoke, the area below deck was deserted, instilling a moment of brief panic as I imagined all kinds of rare seabirds I had missed. I was relieved it was still early, however, and decided that everyone was simply too keen. Still, I didn't want to miss anything so joined the masses on deck (see plate 5).

The hours came and went with the occasional interesting seabird spicing up moments in between. The monotonous sea stretched in every direction, yielding to a continuous bare horizon playing host to the odd distant boat. Onwards we chugged. Then suddenly there was a loud 'Kaboom!!' as Concorde broke the sound barrier somewhere far overhead yet out of sight, – a phenomenon which had fascinated me during the last pelagic when it seemed for a split second that our tiny selected party was being shot at by ghost ships of the Spanish Armada, despite a complete lack of visible vessels (or aircraft for that matter) anywhere within our sights. Now the audio spectacle was less of a surprise and raised few eyebrows amongst a much larger crowd. That great white and majestic bird, now alas forever grounded, boomed out mysteriously in the heavens no less than three times on this particular day, perhaps not quite as loud as when I first heard it back in 1992, but certainly adding to the 'eerie' quality one felt being so far from land.

By 2.00pm, the sun had been beating down mercilessly for some time. There was a brisk, cool breeze over most of the deck but out of the wind, or when it dropped, it really was T-shirt weather. Then again maybe it was better to cover up. I could feel the sunburn already. It was time for a notebook update as by now we had seen quite a few seabirds, including several shearwater species. In fact we were all pretty exhausted, and I felt as if it was time to head back soon. It was very strange the way time itself seemed to have less meaning out here – it was only lunchtime, yet somehow it felt like the day was nearly at an end. Little wonder, I suppose, when you consider that we had already been at sea for some nine hours. By now we were chasing single trawlers (or rather their attendant flocks of hungry seabirds) on the horizon. It was always difficult to judge how far off they were and even more difficult estimating how long it would take to reach them. When we arrived, anticipation would peak, as all eyes strained to scrutinize what birds were in attendance. We would circle the trawler in a large arc, and this had the effect of completely disorientating me. Already feeling 'jet-lagged' and a little out of it with tiredness (not helped by hours of exposure to the hot sun, little to eat and the gentle swaying motion of being on a boat far out at sea), it felt incredibly strange to then lose all sense of direction – a case of feeling dizzy without being dizzy. It made you realize that you usually know 'where's where' – *until* that is, you lose all visual reference points and someone spins you round. It's a good job man-made compasses are more reliable than the body's natural one.

By teatime, things looked bleak. We had seen three Sabine's Gulls and a few Great Shearwaters, but the number of European Storm Petrels (with which Wilson's associates) was lower than usual. Realization was dawning, realization that it would not be fourth time lucky with the infamous Wilson's. We were approaching our last trawler. The glare from the sun on the surface of the sea was strong in places. Conditions were calm and everyone was relaxed; most were resigned to the fact that we were going to see nothing rare today. How wrong we were.

It was almost time to head back, but in the nick of time there was a shout of 'Wilson's Petrel', followed by what seemed like an eternity of mild confusion, a bit of running around on deck and the occasional set of directions called out. It was a tense period while I struggled to connect with it and when I did so, there was another tense period while I waited for better views of the bird. There were some 300 or so birders on the boat making viewing difficult at times. Amidst the frustration, a number of us 'stormed' the upper platform above the control room in a bid to find the best vantage point. In addition the man making announcements over the tannoy on which birds were in view seemed not to know his left from his right! 'Sooty at three o'clock' usually meant 'Sooty at nine o'clock'. Such confusion had been a great source of amusement throughout the day but now it wasn't at all funny. I longed to go back to the days of port and starboard. Then again, this would still confuse half of the birders who would doubtless then run to the wrong side of the boat. At least *they* have an excuse though. There was none for not knowing how to tell the time properly and I began to wonder if the poor sod had his watch on upside-down.

Eventually good views were obtained from the aforementioned platform (see plate 13). By now no one seemed to mind us being up there. 'Mr Enthusiasm' ended up next to me, leaping about and claiming there were four. Maybe he was right, but I was conservative with my later estimate of two or three birds.

And so, at the 11th hour (well probably the 12th or 13th actually), the legendary Petrel had revealed itself. As the boat headed for home, there were more claims of Wilson's, some announced on the tannoy, but no one was too bothered anymore. We had had good views and were not interested in distant 'possibles' that were probably the same birds following us part of the way back. I sat back and smiled, turning my attention to a nice young Swedish girl over from Stockholm for a few days, who was subsequently to become quite a good friend of mine. The sun soon set behind us and that great birding voyage – the quest for Wilson's Petrel – was for me finally over. By now though, I really did have the pelagic 'bug', and the following year saw me hand-feeding Wandering Albatrosses (with incredible three-metre wingspans) from the back of a small boat off New Zealand, as a two-metre Blue Shark, in the hope of a fishy meal, meandered gracefully through the sitting seabirds rocking gently in the swell.

It's not always necessary to take to a boat to see such birds. During onshore winds in late summer and autumn, many shearwaters and petrels are driven close to land and can be seen passing from headland cliff-tops. Porthgwarra, near Land's End in Cornwall, is one such spot and in August 2002, the birds were there a-plenty, as were the birdwatchers, all sat in a small group on the cliff top (see plate 5).

'Excuse me, what are you looking at?' is a phrase well known to any sea-watcher. It falls into the same category as, 'So is there just one of these birds?' and, 'I like a bit of birdwatching m'self' (nudge, nudge, wink, wink), phrases encountered frequently from well-meaning members of the public when they chance upon a bunch of people armed paramilitary-style with optical equipment, cameras, phones and pagers.

When I was asked this question at Porthgwarra I was tempted to reply 'The sea, isn't it beautiful?' or perhaps 'We're checking the horizon for minor deviations from the horizontal plane'. Maybe next time I'll try 'UFOs', 'U-boats' or 'We're trying to see Spain'.

It must look odd, and many people simply cannot comprehend how anyone can want to stare at the sea for so many hours watching little more than dots which pass silently over the water far out in the distance. It can be boring and unpredictable but, under the right conditions, seawatching can also be incredibly exciting and offers observers an excellent chance of finding their own scarce birds. Passing seabirds do not stay around to be twitched and one can expect the unexpected. I love the sea (except when it reminds me of what I've just eaten – I'm no hardened sailor) and there is something special about seeing the birds which spend their lives wandering the open ocean. It was with this in mind that I decided in 2002 to spend a week in Cornwall and the Isles of Scilly with Matthew, a birding friend of mine, during the prime seawatching month of August. On the agenda was some land-based seawatching in Cornwall and as many boat trips as we could fit in.

The trip started badly, taking nearly nine hours to reach Penzance from London. A quick look for Choughs on the Lizard proved fruitless (three wild Choughs reappeared in west Cornwall in spring 2001, probably from the Welsh population, or perhaps even from Ireland, after becoming extinct in the county, whose emblem they are, about 50 years ago). Worst of all, it was announced on our arrival that Sunday's *Scillonian* pelagic, on which we were booked, had been cancelled due to engine failure. The youth hostels in Penzance were crowded and we longed for the B&B I had booked on the Isles of Scilly. When news broke of a male Pallid Harrier, more than 500km away, in Kent, things seemingly could not have got much worse.

Then our luck began to change. The bad weather had brought in seabirds and as it improved over the next few days the light westerlies, occasionally backing south-west, brought in a shearwater bonanza. Small numbers of Sooty, Balearic and Great Shearwaters were passing and on the very first day my 'bogey-bird' fell when I found a Cory's Shearwater passing the Runnel Stone buoy, nearly two kilometres offshore. The first new bird I had found for myself in the UK for many years, it was not particularly awe-inspiring but was closer than the next Cory's which passed shortly afterwards.

The following day I arose at around 4.00am – an hour I didn't think existed. The overcast sky and calm sea provided ideal conditions and by 8.30am I had called the first (and to be the only) Cory's of the day. This one was much better and instantly identifiable, even at a range of nearly two kilometres. Another excellent day's seawatching was had, with similar birds to those seen the day before. We had settled into a pattern of seawatching for a few hours each early morning and again in the evening. These seemed by far the most productive times but, on August 13th, we stuck it out all day, having at one point missed a possible Wilson's Petrel by 15 minutes. Another lone Wilson's was called at around midday and everyone saw the bird, despite the fact that it appeared to be passing somewhere in the vicinity of the continental shelf. At a range of about two kilometres it will only go down in my notebook as a 'possible' but, to be fair, nearly everyone present agreed it was neither Storm (on account of its size) nor Leach's. In fact it was the only storm-type petrel at that range everyone managed to lock onto – even if the views could be compared to locating a speck of dust on the lens of your 'scope and concentrating on it as one panned right over the distant waves. At higher magnification, the speck of dust did however sprout wings. Far more obliging were the dozen or so Small Pearl-bordered Fritillaries (*Boloria selene*) along the approach path, a butterfly I had not seen before.

We next headed for the Isles of Scilly. Halfway across I had already had my best *Scillonian* crossing ever with several Great and Sooty Shearwaters flying near to the boat. As a Great Shearwater swung into our wake, perhaps 200 metres behind us, we followed it with our bins, initially taking little interest in the smaller bird accompanying it. A big mistake. When Matthew said it was another Great, I knew the size and flight action were wrong and that it was worth studying. We had been joined by Andrew Makin, a northern lad travelling to the Isles of Scilly for the same three days we had planned. None of us could initially put a name to the smaller bird, which was still some way off and flying directly towards us. It sheared and towered slightly as it followed the boat. As it banked, we saw the bird side-on for the first time and all noticed a pristine white belly and a very obvious, uniformly dark underwing. Suddenly alarm bells started to ring and I blurted out 'It's a Fea's Petrel!', but by now, it was wheeling south-easterly into the distance. Had we noticed it straight away we surely would have identified it immediately but, as it happened, it became a disappearing dot as we all finally realized what we had just seen and delivered a volley of expletives of varying colour and, sometimes, originality. I phoned in the news as a Great Shearwater appeared close alongside the ship. Soon there were five together. Why hadn't our bird followed them? We would have been laughing – only now we were frustrated that we hadn't had better views. Within minutes of the news being broadcast on the pagers, my phone rang. The call was from a friend stationed at Porthgwarra. 'Keep your eyes peeled,' I told him. 'It might well be coming your way!'

The rest of the day was surreal. We scribbled down a brief description and showed it to several birders based on 'Scilly' who had seen Fea's Petrel previously. All agreed it was one. In fact a distant Fea's-type petrel had been reported flying our way off St Agnes a couple of hours before our sighting – presumably the same bird. We knew we might not have enough of a detailed description to get the record accepted by the British Birds Rarities Committee who vet such claims.

A bit of background on Fea's Petrel might be in order at this point. Although there are no common British species with which it can be confused, it is almost indistinguishable from the exceptionally rare Zino's Petrel (of which there are probably only around 50 pairs in the whole world), so most claims – as was ours – are actually of a Fea's/ Zino's-type. This has not stopped the bird attaining a kind of 'holy grail' status on late summer seawatches in the south-west of Britain and Ireland, however. These birds stormed onto the birding scene as recently as 1989 when the first individuals, wandering from their breeding grounds around the Canaries, were seen off Porthgwarra (there have been only one or two claims pre-dating this). Then known as 'soft-plumaged petrel' the complex was soon afterwards split three ways, incorporating the newly-recognised Fea's and Zino's. Most claims now come from the Scilly pelagics and from the west coast of Ireland. In 2001, one showed well to 300 or so lucky observers on the *Scillonian* pelagic. Anyway, the bottom line is that Fea's Petrels are one of the most sought-after birds amongst British birdwatchers.

That evening we boarded the *Kingfisher* out of St Mary's and headed south. It was a slow start with only a few Great Shearwaters and Storm Petrels. We had been seeing these on a daily basis. Eventually more and more petrels gathered to feed and at last came the cry we had been waiting for: 'Wilson's coming in!' as a rather worn individual glided past the stern and began to feed on the (pleasantly aromatic) 'chum' slick consisting of minced rotten fish and fish/vegetable oil. The bird was joined by another, and then another. One sailed in with a distinctive notch in its wing. Then a blue-phase Fulmar appeared – a rare sighting in these waters. Shortly afterwards, a pristine, newly moulted Wilson's, looking like it had been crafted from velvet, joined the throng. At one point, there were three Wilson's feeding together on the slick. Local birder Bob Flood kept tabs on the numbers, and we finished the evening on a staggering six plus birds, apparently the second highest count ever in British waters, and we were only eight kilometres from St Mary's. But it was the views that made the trip special. The petrels skipped and danced over the waves just ten metres from the boat, sometimes passing within half that distance of the stern. They would then brake sharply and, dangling those long legs and yellow webbed feet, patter away from us over the surface on raised paddle-shaped wings. As the sun set, the petrels became silhouetted against a sea water backdrop of deep blue and pink, perhaps one of my most memorable birding images. It had been a magical day.

The following day, I only managed to glimpse a single Wilson's, and we realized we had been spoilt the night before. But there was another beast I had been secretly hoping for, even though it is seen on average only a couple of times a year from these boats. When it appeared, I simply couldn't believe my luck. I have seen all the British land reptiles but never a Leatherback Turtle (*Dermochelys coriacea*)! I have no idea how big the individual we saw was, but they can grow to some three metres in length and weigh around a tonne. It surely eclipsed those ridiculous pizza-eating Ninja turtles of a few years back – this was the real thing. Even Bob could not believe the luck we were having and no one appreciated this sighting more than me.

On the Friday night, we joined our third and final pelagic trip. Although slightly disappointing in terms of the birds seen, we still managed to observe a few Great Shearwaters and quite incredibly, another Leatherback Turtle. This one was much closer – it appeared from nowhere about 30m from the boat. Andy was still buzzing from having found a Melodious Warbler on St Martin's, and this seemed to complete a fantastic log of amazing wildlife seen…or so we thought.

The day we left the Isles of Scilly was wet and miserable. Taking shelter from the torrential drizzle in a hide at Porth Hellick, we set about counting

Greenshanks and reflecting on the trip. I was watching a couple of Sedge Warblers when another bird suddenly jumped out of a bush to the right of the hide. 'Hippo warbler!' I hissed, referring to the bird's genus *Hippolais*. We were treated to good views of an adult Icterine Warbler for the best part of five minutes. Surely, a most fitting end to the trip at a moment we least expected to see any further new and interesting bird or animal species and, as with everything else on this trip, we had found it ourselves.

The return crossing on the *Scillionian* provided just a few Storm Petrels, a Great Shearwater and a distant Black Tern off the Cornish coast – not to mention enough precipitation from the heavens to extinguish the sun. The following day, Matthew and I drove to Elmley Marshes on the Isle of Sheppey, Kent, where we had excellent views of the Pallid Harrier and both juvenile Marsh Sandpipers recorded as being present there. Birding doesn't get much better than this and these particular few days remain one of my most productive periods of birding ever in these islands.

The Final Fling

By the autumn of 2004, in my quest to see 500 species in the UK and Ireland before I reached the age of 30, I still needed to see another five or six birds, but time was running out. Although an entirely arbitrary goal, its importance had grown in my mind at the same time as its apparent feasibility had decreased, and I became single-minded in the prosecution thereof. I had been attempting to achieve something grand and to fail in my quest suddenly seemed not to be an option, even if the achievement itself had little significance within the context of the rest of the birding scene…and indeed, the affairs of Man. Perhaps it is not the achievement itself that is important, but the taking part. Whatever, I had more adventures during the autumn of 2004 than in any other season. After the relatively quiet autumn of 2003 and the even quieter spring of 2004, I needed a memorable season with lots of new birds and, as things turned out, I was not to be disappointed. Rarities turned up in all parts of the country and time and again, long trips were arranged at very short notice.

With every new bird the pressure increased and the arrangements became stressful. To get to see each new arrival as soon as possible, the cost of a trip usually soared to the point that as so much was invested in travelling to see a given bird, to miss it would simply be intolerable. As companions, I was travelling with some of the most dedicated listers in the country, many of whom would seemingly do almost anything to record a new bird species. They were the same crowd I was used to, but that autumn everyone was pushed to their limits and just a small hardcore group was apparently seeing all the new birds. No doubt, finances, personal relationships and job commitments were being severely tested and a number of keen birders were forced at some point to stay at home. For those that persisted, the rewards were high, but I could not help feeling that at this level the 'tick' is the important thing and the pleasure of seeing the bird is alas secondary. This is perhaps even more the case with year-listing. In recent years, there have been several high profile attempts at breaking the UK and Ireland year list record, some by friends of mine, including the two Adrians – Riley and Webb. I was getting a taste of what it must have been like for them late in the year when every single bird matters and the journeys become more and more ludicrous.

With this amount of pressure, it was perhaps inevitable that I would join the keenest twitchers in the country, but at least for me there was an end in sight. I knew that after my 500th species I might hopefully be able to take a step back and once in a while again be able to say 'no'. For some though, the battle to climb in the rankings continues and, in a few decades time, they may still be at it, trying in a bizarre way to outdo and outlive each other in their battle to be 'top dog'. Nothing wrong with that and good luck to them. Or maybe there is? However, I think that I will just be content to sit somewhere lower down in the rankings and in relative obscurity. Who can say? Perhaps though I have underestimated the addictive nature of this game, and maybe I am naive in thinking I will eventually distance myself from the more extreme element. Despite all such pressure, I have had fun birding at this level and have many fond memories of watching various avifaunal delights going about their business a long way from where they really should be. And that's what it's all about – pleasure from watching a bird.

The 2004 season started with a bang on the 5th September when a Purple Martin, the first ever for Britain, turned up on Lewis, the northernmost island in the Outer Hebrides. The nation's top twitchers had long waited for a new bird and needed little prompting to hotfoot it north. I flew from the north of England in an organized charter on a morning that had my nerves shot to pieces. Initially, there was the traditional 'waiting on news tension' (the martin took a while to be re-discovered), then the problem of getting the deal struck and the plane up in the air in the shortest possible time (see plate 6). En route, we learnt from the pager that a Sparrowhawk had scared it off (the bird, not the plane) – disastrous news indeed. With no sightings of the bird for more than an hour, it was a series of somewhat long faces that approached Lewis in the small chartered aircraft. But then it was found again and panic ensued.

We eventually got to the site of its last known wanderings and there, to our delight, also saw it, spending some two hours watching this rarest of visitors (see plates 6 and 14). As the cloud cleared, more and more Starlings appeared, spiralling upwards in search of the insects that had come out with the warmth. The Martin started ranging widely and eventually disappeared, much to the chagrin of the 50 or so birders who had taken the cheaper option of the ferry. The first of these to arrive missed the bird by an hour. Some birders arrived even later, having paid hundreds of pounds to fly on scheduled flights from Heathrow but there was no further sign of the rare and elusive Martin. It had made a premature departure, disappointing many, and had been seen by perhaps fewer than 50 of us.

I know how these people must have felt, as my next trip was a complete disaster. This time I went for the cheap option of a three-day round trip to Whalsay, Shetland, by ferry from Aberdeen. It was a gruelling journey and gale force winds and rain prevented my companions and me from seeing the bird we had all travelled so far to see – a Brown Shrike. I did voice my suspicions that it was there the whole time but my companions thought that it had simply gone, so we returned home the following day to the news that it was showing again – which just goes to show that you can't win 'em all!

I didn't return to Shetland for the Shrike, which departed soon afterwards anyway. A week later and the Isles of Scilly were flavour of the month with a Cream-coloured Courser on St Agnes, the first in Britain for 20 years. I had a job interview the day after its discovery and was unable to go to look for it, but as luck would have it, not going proved to be the best course of action, or should I say, inaction. Everyone 'dipped' and returned to the mainland in the evening to the news that the bird had just been re-located on the neighbouring island of St Martin's. This time I was available and drove to Penzance overnight from my home in Cambridge. There was some confusion with the flights at the heliport at first light and I ended up taking the *Scillonian III*, the ferry which has served these islands for many years. From St Mary's, I took a smaller boat to St Martin's. Unfortunately, the tide made it impossible to land at the quay and we were transferred to an inflatable, which would have to make three trips. There was a crush on the boat as everyone tried to be part of the first batch to be taken ashore. Luckily, I was on the right side so had little to worry about. The inflatable couldn't bring us all the way to shore, and so it was shoes and socks off as we disembarked in water almost up to our knees and waded to the beach. Apart from one birder falling in, we got ashore safely and made it to see the noble Courser...that is, even after getting lost wandering around St Martin's trying to find the right field in which it temporarily resided. The bird initially played 'hard to get' but when it finally appeared, it was a joy to watch this graceful and charismatic visitor (see plates 15 and 16). It stayed for several weeks – much to the delight of the droves of birders which had booked holidays on the islands during the month of October. Without that particular bird, the 'Scilly season' of 2004 would have gone down as one of the quietest on record for rare birds.

October is well known for its 'purple patches' where a run of several major rarities can turn up in a relatively short period of time. Within a few days of the Cream-coloured Courser being found, several more rarities hit the headlines. First, a Western Sandpiper on Brownsea Island, Poole Harbour, tempted me to make a detour on my return from the Isles of Scilly. I had seen one previously in Ireland but a bird of this rarity at such a convenient location had to be seen to be believed (see plate 15). My next 'port of call' was the RSPB's famous Minsmere reserve in Suffolk where a curlew showing some characters of Slender-billed Curlew (one of the world's rarest birds) had the experts furrowing their brows and searching on hands and knees for droppings so as to be able to test the DNA. This mirrored the occurrence of a previous individual which had been accepted as the first Slender-billed Curlew for Britain, and which I had seen on a return journey home from the Orkney Islands. It would be no tick for me and indeed now appears not to have been the rare species, but it was certainly an educational bird.

It was while I was at this site in Suffolk that news came through of another major rarity, this time on Barra, Western Isles. In recent years a pioneering group of birders had been working there regularly in October to investigate its rarity potential. They had hypothesized that not only was the island in a good westerly position for receiving American vagrants directly, but that it might also receive birds which had been displaced to the island chain further north and which would attempt to move south (as most migratory birds do at this time of year). Barra is considerably smaller than these other islands and suitably barren. Vegetation is concentrated in a handful of small areas, therefore presumably making birds easier to find. In short, it was a 'workable' island, which offered the last area of shelter in the Hebrides for birds moving south and was as such a bottleneck that might just hold a few surprises at this time of year. And hold surprises it did – a whole host of rarities were discovered, but it was only during the visiting birders' third visit, in 2004, that the first 'mega' was found. The bird was a Yellow Warbler and I was determined to see it. This one was personal after I had been 'stood up' by the last to occur, some nine years earlier. On that occasion, an unfortunate chain of events, which unraveled after I had stumbled from a student party near my home, then in North Wales, led to me missing the bird by just an hour and a half. Had I caught the bus from Dublin as I had intended, I would then almost certainly have been luckier and actually seen it, but it wasn't to be. And now, here I was planning a trip to Barra that would not be straightforward.

The first set of plans involved chartering two light aircraft from the north of England. These plans fell through when it was revealed that we would have to pay to open Benbecula Airport for the occasion! This only came to light late in the evening and by then most had given up on getting there by the following day. I did make it eventually but not on a chartered plane. The plans were renewed for the following day but, with storm-force winds forecast, I didn't think the aircraft would actually take off. I arranged to fly on a scheduled flight from Glasgow via Benbecula, yet narrowly missed the last two seats available on a direct (and much cheaper) flight. The weather conditions during my two flights were horrendous and, as there is no purpose-built runway on Barra, we had to land on the beach (see plate 5). Apparently this is the only airport in the world with such arrangements; it does mean of course that landing is restricted to a few hours a day around low tide. With only two hours of daylight left in which to see the bird it was yet another race against time. Gale force winds and rain had got the better of me on Shetland but luckily they didn't bother the Yellow Warbler. It was showing on my arrival and I barely waited for my transport to stop before I disembarked, practically falling out of the vehicle in my haste to see the bird. A showy little blighter, it continued to delight a small but steady stream of admirers over the following days (see plate 15). As with many twitches, the dashing turned out not to be necessary but, on the other hand, you never can tell.

After the Yellow Warbler, the birding community was able to enjoy a much-needed rest. A 'Greenland Redpoll' tempted me to make a trip to the Isles of Scilly but this hasn't yet officially been given full specific status and, although the guidelines I was following allow it to be counted, I couldn't quite come round to the idea for travelling so far for such a bird. A possible 'Caspian' Reed Warbler, also on the Isles of Scilly, further tempted me. With these two birds in the hand, I would have my 500 total but I was now suffering a crisis of conscience. I felt a sudden desire to revert back to the official guidelines of the British Ornithologists' Union (BOU). I wasn't quite sure if I agreed with one or two of the 'unofficial' decisions being made by the UK400 Club on these, and certain other birds. The tick-hungry twitcher within me was giving way to the more cautious scientist. I wanted to see the birds on the Isles of Scilly – no doubt about that as such birds are educational if nothing else – but wasn't prepared to make such a long trip for birds I wasn't happy about counting in my total. I prayed something better would turn up, and on the 16th of October, my prayers were answered.

Here there was more controversy though. Not on taxonomic grounds this time but on origin. The bird in question, a Chestnut-eared Bunting on Fair Isle, was a potential Western Palaearctic first (see plate 16). The bird is found in the wild no nearer to the UK than Kashmir. In itself this means little but, being a mainly short distance migrant, the likelihood of it being an escaped cage-bird was very real. I had to consider the points for and against the likelihood of natural origin – location, date, age of the bird, condition, likelihood of vagrancy and status in captivity. When I had considered all, I got straight on the phone and chartered a plane to take me and a handful of others to Fair Isle the following day.

The debate raged for weeks, and it is sad to think that this bird will probably never be fully accepted onto the British list thanks to the uncertainty of its origin. My opinion may be biased, but I firmly believe that this record truly relates to a wild bird. Taxonomy and origin remain the most fiercely debated topics within birding and can make listing far from straightforward. It is these issues that create a gulf between the official guidelines of the BOU and the unofficial ones of the UK400 Club, which I, despite some reservations, had decided to follow. My other highlight from that day on Fair Isle was the sight of a flock of 17 Bullfinches of one of the Siberian races, showing at a range of just a few metres (see plate 15). There may be few calling for these to be 'split' (named species in their own right), but that didn't detract from the magic of watching these stunning birds with their delightfully distinctive 'toy trumpet' nasal calls, rather different to the sounds made by British Bullfinches. It was like seeing the northern race Long-tailed Tits in Suffolk earlier in the year – no tick but well worth the trip for the magic of seeing a flock of such charming birds.

Just a week later, Fair Isle was calling again with another Western Palaearctic first – a Rufous-tailed Robin. I turned down the offer of a seat on a flight from the north of England and instead arranged a charter flight of my own the following morning from Wick in Scotland. Having been pampered using charters from the south, it was a long time since I had been in a car for so long, but this is how it was done until just a few years ago. As it turned out, the bird wasn't present on the day we travelled and we dipped out. The return journey took 24 hours, of which around 18 were spent travelling. Apparently, there were so many birders at one airport down south that three small planes had to start off at first light before it was known whether the bird was even present. Otherwise not everyone would have made it that day. When it was clear that the 'bird had flown', the planes landed at separate airports – Aberdeen, Dundee and Glasgow. Two returned home but one became grounded in bad weather. So, although we had had a bad day, others had fared worse.

I managed a day of recovery before being 'called off' again, this time to the Isles of Scilly for – believe it or not – an Ovenbird. Ovenbird is another bird species that had never previously been available long enough for the birding community to catch up with. It is a delightful little ground-dwelling warbler from North America that had occurred on just three previous occasions in Britain and Ireland. It was a very much sought-after species, following a suppressed individual in a Midlands' back garden the year before and a bird present for two days in south-west Ireland in 1990.

I was on the phone all afternoon. Birders jammed the lines of the travel centres, booking planes and helicopters to the islands the following day. The Skybus office was engaged solidly for about two hours. By then, all flights had been fully booked. It was the same story with the helicopters. Ringing a friend of mine, I was astonished to hear that he was already on the Isles of Scilly. I had bumped into him in a lay-by between Inverness and Wick, just two days earlier. It turned out that he had been at Land's End, Cornwall, when news of the Ovenbird had broken, and had got straight across on a flight. Apparently, he had been staying at Land's End and had driven up to Wick for the Robin, before returning to Land's End to continue birding this area. That's a hell of a lot of mileage. I rang Adrian Webb and heard that he had booked a private plane to fly from the north of England to Southend in Essex to collect him and his Dad and then onwards to the Isles of Scilly. These were desperate and expensive measures to get himself and pater there that day in case the bird departed. A third birder had boarded the same plane further north at a staggering cost of £900. They got there before dusk but the bird had disappeared just minutes beforehand.

The panic, as it turned out, was largely unnecessary. The Ovenbird stayed for several days and even the following day, everyone who wished to see it managed to get across, some using just a fleeting day return visit to the islands on the passenger ferry, the *Scillonian*. Tides that day dictated that the 'day return' gave less than two hours on the islands, which is not that much time to catch up with an elusive bird like an Ovenbird (it had disappeared for more than three hours the previous day). I booked a private plane from the South-West and had a great day with exceptionally close views of the bird (see plate 15). Unafraid of humans, it approached me to within a few metres as I lay on my stomach watching it and it walked to within arm's reach of some of the photographers. I managed to fit in a mini-twitch to a neighbouring island for a Swainson's Thrush, but the bird proved elusive in the extreme and I failed to see it in the hour and a half available to me.

The autumn finished with a bang when a Masked Shrike – the first ever for Britain – turned up in Fife and, on October 31st, I paid my respects to this most showy of birds (see plate 15). I was actually still buzzing from having found, with a friend of mine, Cambridgeshire's second ever Pacific Golden Plover the day before amongst a 3,000-strong flock of Golden Plover on my 'local patch' in the fens. A find like that only happens (in my experience) every few years, so it had been a bumper autumn in every respect.

A sad post-script comes in the form of the news that the two birds on the Isles of Scilly – the Cream-coloured Courser and Ovenbird – became ill and were taken into care. Both died almost immediately, within 24 hours of each other. Unfortunately, this is the likely fate of many rare birds reaching the UK, although they usually expire well away from prying eyes. It is generally assumed that for every bird that crosses to Britain from North America and makes a landfall, there are many more which don't make it and drop into the ocean.

Pacific golden plover

So my 500th species (UK400 rules) became Masked Shrike and it was on this total that I celebrated my thirtieth birthday in December 2004. It marked the end to my busiest-ever birding season and perhaps the most expensive one to the keenest of the twitching community. There had been more major rarities than normal and they had all been on outlying islands – right up until the Masked Shrike turned up in mainland Scotland (see plate 7). In less than two months during the autumn, I had covered nearly 10,000km and my expenditure ran a long way into four figures. There had been an average of one long-distance trip a week with much of the intervening periods spent birding 'local patches' close to my home in Cambridgeshire.

My next goal will be to see 500 species from the official BOU British list, which will probably take another few years, and so far has only been achieved by a few dozen committed individuals with at least a ten year head start on me. During this time, I hope to continue to search areas close to my home for local rarities and should hopefully learn much more about bird identification, vagrancy and behaviour. Since the natural world so fascinates me, I will also continue my quest to encounter other forms of wildlife in the British Isles, spending time pursuing (if that's the word) and photographing a few select mammal species in particular, not to mention an elusive butterfly species (Chequered Skipper, *Carterocephalus palaemon* – the only British butterfly of the 60 or so species which has managed to elude me to date in Britain) and some of the non-native amphibians we have here.

I have already undertaken a number of long-distance car journeys in Britain at a moment's notice to see, for example, various whales for the pleasure of watching and learning more about them. Cetaceans, bats, butterflies, moths, marine fish and turtles all have the capacity to turn up here a long way from their native areas, although in much smaller numbers than birds do (except perhaps the fish, but who can twitch them? World shark-listing – now *there's* an idea!). More and more birders these days are expanding their interests to other forms of wildlife. As there are fewer new birds to see in Britain and Ireland, they start to learn about insects in particular and there is even a long-standing community of orchid-twitchers, willing to travel long distances at very short notice…that is, before the flower spikes have shown their all and died off. Despite the greatly increased chances of success, I have, however, instructed various friends to strap me to a chair and slap me about the face with a wet fish if I ever talk about hiring a plane and travelling a thousand kilometres to see a plant.

Post Script

In April 2005, an exotic-looking Belted Kingfisher became bird number 501 on my British/Irish list. It turned up on April 1st, and was dismissed by many as an April Fool's Day hoax, due to the exceptional rarity of the bird (the second for Britain and the first for some 25 years), the unlikely location (Staffordshire) and the fact that it had been reported by just one person with no subsequent sightings for many hours. When birders realised their mistake (myself included), those who hadn't made it to see the bird on its first day turned up the next. Despite perhaps 1,000 observers being present, there was no kingfisher...at least until the afternoon when it was reported about 120km away in Yorkshire. A mass convoy of folk then quickly motored north-east...but it was to no avail: the bird had already flown.

A few days later came the incredible news that the same bird had turned up near Aberdeen on its continuing northerly migration. I was unable to go for two days due to an imminent job interview. Fortunately, and to my immense relief, it was still present on the Friday morning, when I took the photograph shown (see plate 16). Hundreds of people journeyed up north on Friday night, yet it was reportedly seen by just two of them...very briefly at dawn the following day, before disappearing without a trace.

Also in 2005 an albatross was discovered in a largely inaccessible gannet colony at Sula Sgeir, North of the Western Isles. It is thought the bird may well be Albert, who would now be at least 45 years of age, with increased longevity perhaps a result of this unfortunate individual's failure to breed.

Bird sightings mentioned in the text

Birds marked with an asterisk (*) are considered rarities under the official rules of the British Birds Rarities Committee (as of December 2005). Common name, scientific name, location and details of sighting are listed.

1. **Greenland White-fronted Goose** *Anas flavirostris*
   Wexford North Slob; large flock on 27th October 2002
2. ***King Eider,*** *Somateria spectabilis*
   Burra Sound, Shetland; 29th June 1997
3. **Red-throated Diver,** *Gavia stellata*
   Hermaness, Shetland; 14th April 1993
4. **Great Northern Diver,** *Gavia immer*
   Carnsore Point, Co Wexford; 2 on 27th October 2002
5. ***Black-browed Albatross,*** *Thalassarche melanophris*
   Hermaness, Shetland; 14th April 1993
6. **Northern Fulmar,** *Fulmarus glacialis*
   *c.*10km south of St Mary's, Isles of Scilly; 'blue phase' bird on 14th August 2002; others encountered mainly when seawatching and during pelagic trips
7. ***Fea's Petrel,*** *Pterodroma feae*
   *c.*25km east of Isles of Scilly, 1 from the *Scillonian* en route to Isles of Scilly, 14th August 2002
8. **Cory's Shearwater,** *Calonectris diomedea*
   Porthgwarra, Cornwall; 3 birds seen on 11th-12th August 2002 with 2 possibles on the 13th
9. **Great Shearwater,** *Puffinus gravis*
   Cornwall, Isles of Scilly & South-Western Approaches; at least 45 seen 11th-17th August 2002 from Porthgwarra, Cornwall, west to St Mary's, Isles of Scilly; 8+ seen on *Scillonian* pelagic, 16th August 1998
10. **Sooty Shearwater,** *Puffinus griseus*
    Porthgwarra, Cornwall, west to St Mary's, Isles of Scilly & South-Western Approaches; 37 seen 11th-16th August 2002

11. **Balearic Shearwater,** *Puffinus mauretanicus*
    Cornwall, Isles of Scilly & South-Western Approaches; 20+ seen in Porthgwarra, Cornwall, 11th-13th August 2002; 2 from the *Scillonian* pelagic, 16th August 1998
12. ***Wilson's Storm-petrel,** *Oceanites oceanicus*
    Cornwall, Isles of Scilly & South-Western Approaches; 2-3, possibly 4, on *Scillonian* pelagic, 16th August 1998; possible off Porthgwarra, Cornwall, 13th August 2002; at least 6, *c.*10km south of St Mary's, Isles of Scilly on 14th August 2002 with another nearby on 15th
13. **European Storm-petrel,** *Hydrobates pelagicus*
    Porthgwarra, Cornwall, west to St Mary's, Isles of Scilly, *Scillonian* pelagic & South-Western Approaches; 100+ seen 11th-17th August 2002, 150+ on 16th August 1998
14. **Northern Gannet,** *Morus bassanus*
    Hermaness, Shetland; many, 14th April 1993; also encountered on most of the seawatches and pelagics in the South-West (see Chapter 12)
15. ***Black Kite,** *Milvus migrans*
    Setter Farm, Yell, Shetland; 27th-29th June 1997
16. **Hen Harrier,** *Circus cyaneus*
    Wexford North Slob, Co Wexford; 27th October 2002
17. ***Pallid Harrier***, *Circus macrourus*
    Elmley, Isle of Sheppey, Kent; 18th August 2002
18. **Common Buzzard,** *Buteo buteo*
    Stornoway, Isle of Lewis; 26th October 1998; common species, often seen in transit on birding trips
19. **Peregrine,** *Falco peregrinus*
    Wexford North Slob, Co Wexford; 27th October 2002
20. **Common Crane,** *Grus grus*
    Fair Isle, Shetland; 3rd-4th June 1998
21. ***Cream-coloured Courser,** *Cursorius cursor*
    St Martin's, Isles of Scilly; 30th September 2004
22. **Eurasian Dotterel,** *Charadrius morinellus*
    Fair Isle, Shetland; 4th June 1998

23. ***Pacific Golden Plover,** *Pluvialis fulva*
    Fidwell Fen, Cambs; 30th October 2004
24. ***Western Sandpiper,** *Calidris mauri*
    Brownsea Island, Poole Harbour; 1st October 2004
25. ***Slender-billed Curlew,** *Numenius tenuirostris*
    Druridge Pools, Northumberland, 6th May 1998
26. **Eurasian Curlew,** *Numenius arquata*
    Minsmere, Suffolk; 2nd October 2004; seen frequently on birding trips in the appropriate habitat
27. ***Marsh Sandpiper,** *Tringa stagnatilis*
    Elmley, Isle of Sheppey, Kent; 2 on 18th August 2002
28. **Common Greenshank,** *Tringa nebularia*
    Porth Hellick Pool, St Mary's, Isles of Scilly; 8 on 17th August 2002; seen regularly on other trips
29. **Red-necked Phalarope,** *Phalaropus lobatus*
    Fetlar, Shetland; 4-5 breeding pairs on 27th June 1997,
30. **Great Skua** ('bonxie'), *Stercorarius skua*
    Hermaness, Shetland; several on 14th April 1993. Also regular on seawatches and pelagics in the South-West (see Chapter 12) and on Shetland during the summer months
31. **Sabine's Gull,** *Larus sabini*
    South-Western Approaches; 3 on 16th August 1998
32. **Iceland Gull,** *Larus glaucoides*
    Brei Wick, Shetland; 31st March 1992
33. **Black Tern,** *Chlidonias niger*
    Off Porthgwarra, Cornwall; 17th August 2002
34. ***Elegant Tern,** *Sterna elegans*
    Dingle, Co Kerry (Ireland); 26th October 2002
35. **Sandwich Tern,** *Sterna sandvicensis*
    Carnsore Point, Co Wexford (Ireland); 30+ on 27th October 2002; encountered often on birding trips outside the winter months
36. ***Lesser-crested Tern,** *Sterna bengalensis*
    Scolt Head Island, Norfolk; July 1993

37. **Arctic Tern,** *Sterna paradisaea*
    Setter Farm, Yell, Shetland; 29th June 1997; encountered frequently in certain places like Shetland during the summer
38. **Razorbill,** *Alca torda*
    Jenny's Cove, Lundy, Devon; many, 24th April 1991
39. ***Ancient Murrelet,** *Synthliboramphus antiquus*
    Jenny's Cove, Lundy, Devon; 24th April 1991
40. **Little Auk,** *Alle alle*
    Crossing to Lewis, Western Isles; 26th October 1998
41. **Atlantic Puffin,** *Fratercula arctica*
    Hermaness, Shetland; many, 14th April 1993
42. ***Alpine Swift,** *Apus melba*
    Fair Isle, Shetland; 30th September 2002
43. ***Belted Kingfisher,** *Ceryle alcyon*
    Peterculter, Aberdeenshire; 8th April 2005
44. ***Blue-cheeked Bee-eater,** *Merops persicus*
    Asta House, Shetland mainland; 27th June 1997
45. ***Purple Martin,** *Progne subis*
    Europie, (Butt of Lewis), Western Isles; 6th September 2004
46. **Barn Swallow,** *Hirundo rustica*
    Carnsore Point, Co Wexford; 27th October 2002; summer visitor seen on most birding trips, mainly April - October
47. **Richard's Pipit,** *Anthus richardi*
    Fair Isle, Shetland; 18th October 2003
48. ***Pechora Pipit,** *Anthus gustavi*
    Fair Isle, Shetland; 28th September & 5th October 2002
49. ***Red-throated Pipit,** *Anthus cervinus*
    Fair Isle, Shetland; 5th June 1998
50. ***Gray Catbird,** *Dumetella caraolinensis*
    South Stack, Holyhead, Anlesey; 5th October 2001
51. ***Siberian Rubythroat,** *Luscinia calliope*
    Osmington Mill, Dorset & Fair Isle, Shetland; 19th October 1997 and 18th October 2003, respectively
52. **Bluethroat,** *Luscinia svecica*
    Fair Isle, Shetland; 4th June 1998

53. **Northern Wheatear,** *Oenanthe oenanthe*
    Carnsore Point, Co Wexford; 27th October 2002; reasonably common, seen regularly on birding trips
54. ***White's Thrush,** *Zoothera dauma*
    North Tolsta, Isle of Lewis & Fair Isle, Shetland; 26th October 1998 & 29th September 2002, respectively
55. **Ring Ouzel,** *Turdus torquatus*
    Hermaness, Shetland; several, 14th April 1993
56. ***American Robin,** *Turdus migratorius*
    St Agnes, Isles of Scilly & Grimsby, Lincs; 28th October 1998 & 9th and 11th January 2004, respectively
57. **Sedge Warbler,** *Acrocephalus schoenobaenus*
    Porth Hellick Pool, St Mary's, Isles of Scilly; 2 on 17th August 2002; often encountered during birding in the summer months
58. **Icterine Warbler,** *Hippolais icterina*
    Porth Hellick Pool, St Mary's, Isles of Scilly & Lerwick, Shetland; 17th August 2002 & 28th June 1997, respectively
59. ***Radde's Warbler,** *Phylloscopus schwarzi*
    St Levan, Cornwall; 19th October 1997
60. **Red-backed Shrike,** *Lanius collurio*
    Virkie, Shetland; 29th June 1997; Fair Isle, Shetland; 3, 3rd-6th June 1998
61. ***Masked Shrike,** *Lanius nubicus*
    Kilrenny, Fife; 31st October 2004
62. **Common Raven,** *Corvus corax*
    Hermaness, Shetland; several on 14th April 1993; seen regularly during birding trips, especially in the north and west.
63. **Common Starling,** *Sturnus vulgaris*
    North Tolsta, Isle of Lewis; 2 on 26th October 1998; a very common species seen at some point on most birding trips
64. ***Spanish Sparrow,** *Passer hispaniolensis*
    Waterside, Cumbria; 29th June 1997
65. **House Sparrow,** *Passer domesticus*
    Fair Isle, Shetland; small flock on 18th October 2003; a very common species seen at some point on most birding trips

66. **European Greenfinch,** *Carduelis chloris*
    Fair Isle, Shetland; small flock on 18th October 2003; a very common species seen at some point on most birding trips
67. ***Pine Grosbeak,** *Pinicola enucleator*
    Lerwick, Shetland; 31st March 1992
68. **Common Bullfinch,** *Pyrrhula pyrrhula*
    Fair Isle, Shetland; 17 Eastern race birds on 17th October 2004
69. ***Blue-winged Warbler,** *Vermivora pinus*
    Cape Clear, Co Cork (Ireland); 4th October 2000
70. ***Golden-winged Warbler,** *Vermivora chrysoptera*
    Larkfield, Kent; 11th February 1989
71. ***Yellow Warbler,** *Dendroica petechia*
    Barra, Western Isles; 4th-5th October 2004
72. ***Blackpoll Warbler,** *Dendroica striata*
    Tresco, Scilly; 13th October 1997
73. ***Ovenbird,** *Seiurus aurocapillus*
    Trenoweth, St Mary's, Isles of Scilly; 26th October 2004
74. ***Common Yellowthroat,** *Geothlypis trichas*
    St Mary's, Isles of Scilly; 12th October 1997
75. ***Savannah Sparrow,** *Passerculus sandwichensis*
    Fair Isle, Shetland; 18th October 2003
76. **Chestnut-eared Bunting,** *Emberiza fucata*
    Fair Isle, Shetland; 17th October 2004
77. ***Rustic Bunting,** *Emberiza rustica*
    Beddington Sewage Farm, Greater London; 20th February 1993

Listing – the technical stuff

Listing birds, although a simple concept, is in practice fraught with difficulty. Some birders keep their own list, but most follow official guidelines. The official British list is kept by the British Ornithologists' Union (BOU) and as of March 2006, stands at some 572 species. The Irish list is kept by the Irish Rare Birds Committee (IRBC). As the BOU are a scientific body, a considerable amount of research from around the world is analysed before decisions regarding the admission of birds onto the country list are made. This list is after all definitive, recognized by the law of the land in matters relating to conservation and wildlife crime. Many birders are however put off by what they see as a conservative approach (even when compared to some other countries' rarities committees) and decisions that sometimes come seemingly years late, although this situation has improved. The BOU's task is not an enviable one, however, its records committee (BOURC) must judge whether a potentially new bird for Britain is likely to be wild and not from some zoo or collection. It must decide whether it has been identified correctly and, perhaps most difficult of all, whether it really should be classed as a full species (as opposed to a sub-species or racial variant). This is why decisions take time and part of the reason for the formation of the UK400 Club was to provide an alternative set of guidelines, and it is these on which the list below is based.

These guidelines are still based on research and only made after widespread collaboration but are often criticized for being unscientific with undemocratic decisions, the ultimate say being down to one person (Lee Evans, the club's founder). The club may be controversial but the decisions are more up to speed and more likely to 'give the bird the benefit of the doubt' if, say, it can't be proven whether the bird is a genuine wild vagrant or whether it could have hopped out of its pen at some zoo. These guidelines are thus sometimes considered more user-friendly for listing purposes. It should be said though, that part of their attraction for some may be that they significantly help increase birders' lists! There are 27 birds listed below which have not yet been accepted (or recognized as full species) onto the respective country lists by either the BOURC or the

IRBC (these are marked with an asterisk* and most relate to records still under review). There are two further species (Slender-billed Curlew, *Numenius tenuirostris* and Scottish Crossbill, *Loxia scotica*) recognised by the BOU and seen by the author in Britain that are not recognised by the UK400 Club. For the sake of continuity/conformity, these two are not listed below, despite the author's opinion that the curlew should be included.

The advantage of having two sets of guidelines of course is that the author – and many others – get to celebrate seeing 500 birds twice! Well, one lives in hope…

The total list (as of December 2005)

1. **Mute Swan**, *Cygnus olor*
2. **Tundra (Bewick's) Swan**, *Cygnus columbianus*
3. **Whooper Swan**, *Cygnus cygnus*
4. **Bean Goose**, *Anser fabalis*
5. ***Tundra Bean Goose**, *Anser rossicus*
6. **Pink-footed Goose**, *Anser brachyrhynchus*
7. **Greater White-fronted Goose**, *Anser albifrons*
8. ***Greenland White-fronted Goose**, *Anser flavirostris*
9. **Lesser White-fronted Goose**, *Anser erythropus*
10. **Greylag Goose**, *Anser anser*
11. **Snow Goose**, *Anser caerulescens*
12. ***Ross's Goose**, *Anser rossii*
13. **Greater Canada Goose**, *Branta canadensis*
14. **Lesser Canada Goose**, *Branta hutchinsii*
15. **Barnacle Goose**, *Branta leucopsis*
16. **Dark-bellied Brent Goose**, *Branta bernicla*
17. ***Pale-bellied Brent Goose**, *Branta hrota*
18. ***Black Brant**, *Branta nigricans*
19. **Red-breasted Goose**, *Branta ruficollis*
20. **Egyptian Goose**, *Alopochen aegyptiacus*
21. **Ruddy Shelduck**, *Tadorna ferruginea*
22. **Common Shelduck**, *Tadorna tadorna*
23. **Mandarin Duck**, *Aix galericulata*
24. **Eurasian Wigeon**, *Anas penelope*

25. **American Wigeon**, *Anas americana*
26. ***Marbled Duck**, *Marmaronetta angustirostris*
27. ***Falcated Duck**, *Anas falcata*
28. **Gadwall**, *Anas strepera*
29. **Eurasian Teal**, *Anas crecca*
30. **Green-winged Teal**, *Anas carolinensis*
31. **Mallard**, *Anas platyrhynchos*
32. **American Black Duck**, *Anas rubripes*
33. **Northern Pintail**, *Anas acuta*
34. **Garganey**, *Anas querquedula*
35. **Blue-winged Teal**, *Anas discors*
36. ***Baikal Teal**, *Anas formosa*
37. ***Cinnamon Teal**, *Anas cyanoptera*
38. **Northern Shoveler**, *Anas clypeata*
39. **Red-crested Pochard**, *Netta rufina*
40. **Common Pochard**, *Aythya ferina*
41. **Redhead**, *Aythya americana*
42. **Canvasback**, *Aythya valisineria*
43. **Ring-necked Duck**, *Aythya collaris*
44. **Ferruginous Duck**, *Aythya nyroca*
45. **Tufted Duck**, *Aythya fuligula*
46. **Greater Scaup**, *Aythya marila*
47. **Lesser Scaup**, *Aythya affinis*
48. **Common Eider**, *Somateria mollissima*
49. **King Eider**, *Somateria spectabilis*
50. **Steller's Eider**, *Polysticta stelleri*
51. **Harlequin Duck**, *Histrionicus histrionicus*
52. **Long-tailed Duck**, *Clangula hyemalis*
53. **Common Scoter**, *Melanitta nigra*
54. **Black Scoter**, *Melanitta americana*
55. **Surf Scoter**, *Melanitta perspicillata*
56. **Velvet Scoter**, *Melanitta fusca*
57. **Bufflehead**, *Bucephala albeola*
58. **Barrow's Goldeneye**, *Bucephala islandica*
59. **Common Goldeneye**, *Bucephala clangula*
60. **Smew**, *Mergellus albellus*
61. **Red-breasted Merganser**, *Mergus serrator*
62. **Goosander**, *Mergus merganser*
63. ***Hooded Merganser**, *Lophodytes cucullatus*
64. **Ruddy Duck**, *Oxyura jamaicensis*

65. ***White-headed Duck,** *Oxyura leucocephala*
66. **WillowPtarmigan,** *Lagopus lagopus*
67. **Rock Ptarmigan,** *Lagopus muta*
68. **Black Grouse,** *Tetrao tetrix*
69. **Western Capercaillie,** *Tetrao urogallus*
70. **Red-legged Partridge,** *Alectoris rufa*
71. **Grey Partridge,** *Perdix perdix*
72. **Common Quail,** *Coturnix coturnix*
73. **Common Pheasant,** *Phasianus colchicus*
74. **Golden Pheasant,** *Chrysolophus pictus*
75. **Lady Amherst's Pheasant,** *Chrysolophus amherstiae*
76. **Red-throated Diver,** *Gavia stellata*
77. **Black-throated Diver,** *Gavia arctica*
78. **Great Northern Diver,** *Gavia immer*
79. **Yellow-billed Diver,** *Gavia adamsii*
80. **Pied-billed Grebe,** *Podilymbus podiceps*
81. **Little Grebe,** *Tachybaptus ruficollis*
82. **Great Crested Grebe,** *Podiceps cristatus*
83. **Red-necked Grebe,** *Podiceps grisegena*
84. **Slavonian Grebe,** *Podiceps auritus*
85. **Black-necked Grebe,** *Podiceps nigricollis*
86. **Black-browed Albatross,** *Thalassarche melanophris*
87. **Common Fulmar,** *Fulmarus glacialis*
88. **Fea's Petrel,** *Pterodroma feae*
89. **Cory's Shearwater,** *Calonectris diomedea*
90. **Great Shearwater,** *Puffinus gravis*
91. **Sooty Shearwater,** *Puffinus griseus*
92. **Manx Shearwater,** *Puffinus puffinus*
93. **Balearic Shearwater,** *Puffinus mauretanicus*
94. **Wilson's Storm-petrel,** *Oceanites oceanicus*
95. **European Storm-petrel,** *Hydrobates pelagicus*
96. **Leach's Storm-petrel,** *Oceanodroma leucorhoa*
97. **Northern Gannet,** *Morus bassanus*
98. **Great Cormorant,** *Phalacrocorax carbo*
99. **Double-crested Cormorant,** *Phalacrocorax auritus*
100. **European Shag,** *Phalacrocorax aristotelis*

101. **Great Bittern**, *Botaurus stellaris*
102. **American Bittern**, *Botaurus lentiginosus*
103. **Little Bittern**, *Ixobrychus minutus*
104. **Black-crowned Night Heron**, *Nycticorax nycticorax*
105. **Green Heron**, *Butorides virescens*
106. **Squacco Heron**, *Ardeola ralloides*
107. **Cattle Egret**, *Bubulcus ibis*
108. **Little Egret**, *Egretta garzetta*
109. **Snowy Egret**, *Egretta thula*
110. **Great Egret**, *Ardea alba*
111. **Grey Heron**, *Ardea cinerea*
112. **Purple Heron**, *Ardea purpurea*
113. **Black Stork**, *Ciconia nigra*
114. **White Stork**, *Ciconia ciconia*
115. **Glossy Ibis**, *Plegadis falcinellus*
116. **Eurasian Spoonbill**, *Platalea leucorodia*
117. *****Greater Flamingo**, *Phoenicopterus ruber*
118. **European Honey-buzzard**, *Pernis apivorus*
119. **Black Kite**, *Milvus migrans*
120. **Red Kite**, *Milvus milvus*
121. **White-tailed Eagle**, *Haliaeetus albicilla*
122. **Eurasian Marsh Harrier**, *Circus aeruginosus*
123. **Hen Harrier**, *Circus cyaneus*
124. **Pallid Harrier**, *Circus macrourus*
125. **Montagu's Harrier**, *Circus pygargus*
126. **Northern Goshawk**, *Accipiter gentilis*
127. **Eurasian Sparrowhawk**, *Accipiter nisus*
128. **Common Buzzard**, *Buteo buteo*
129. **Rough-legged Buzzard**, *Buteo lagopus*
130. **Golden Eagle**, *Aquila chrysaetos*
131. **Osprey**, *Pandion haliaetus*
132. **Lesser Kestrel**, *Falco naumanni*
133. **Common Kestrel**, *Falco tinnunculus*
134. **Red-footed Falcon**, *Falco vespertinus*
135. **Merlin**, *Falco columbarius*
136. **Eurasian Hobby**, *Falco subbuteo*
137. **Gyr Falcon**, *Falco rusticolus*
138. **Peregrine Falcon**, *Falco peregrinus*
139. **Water Rail**, *Rallus aquaticus*
140. **Spotted Crake**, *Porzana porzana*
141. **Sora**, *Porzana carolina*
142. **Little Crake**, *Porzana parva*
143. **Corn Crake**, *Crex crex*
144. **Common Moorhen**, *Gallinula chloropus*
145. **Common Coot**, *Fulica atra*

146. **American Coot**, *Fulica americana*
147. **Common Crane**, *Grus grus*
148. **Little Bustard**, *Tetrax tetrax*
149. **Eurasian Oystercatcher**, *Haematopus ostralegus*
150. **Black-winged Stilt**, *Himantopus himantopus*
151. **Pied Avocet**, *Recurvirostra avosetta*
152. **Stone-curlew**, *Burhinus oedicnemus*
153. **Cream-coloured Courser**, *Cursorius cursor*
154. **Collared Pratincole**, *Glareola pratincola*
155. **Oriental Pratincole**, *Glareola maldivarum*
156. **Black-winged Pratincole**, *Glareola nordmanni*
157. **Little Plover**, *Charadrius dubius*
158. **Ringed Plover**, *Charadrius hiaticula*
159. **Semipalmated Plover**, *Charadrius semipalmatus*
160. **Killdeer**, *Charadrius vociferus*
161. **Kentish Plover**, *Charadrius alexandrinus*
162. **Lesser Sand Plover**, *Charadrius mongolus*
163. **Greater Sand Plover**, *Charadrius leschenaultii*
164. **Eurasian Dotterel**, *Charadrius morinellus*
165. **American Golden Plover**, *Pluvialis dominica*
166. **Pacific Golden Plover**, *Pluvialis fulva*
167. **European Golden Plover**, *Pluvialis apricaria*
168. **Grey Plover**, *Pluvialis squatarola*
169. **Sociable Lapwing**, *Vanellus gregarius*
170. **Northern Lapwing**, *Vanellus vanellus*
171. **Great Knot**, *Calidris tenuirostris*
172. **Red Knot**, *Calidris canutus*
173. **Sanderling**, *Calidris alba*
174. **Semipalmated Sandpiper**, *Calidris pusilla*
175. **Western Sandpiper**, *Calidris mauri*
176. **Red-necked Stint**, *Calidris ruficollis*
177. **Little Stint**, *Calidris minuta*
178. **Temminck's Stint**, *Calidris temminckii*
179. **Least Sandpiper**, *Calidris minutilla*
180. **White-rumped Sandpiper**, *Calidris fuscicollis*
181. **Baird's Sandpiper**, *Calidris bairdii*
182. **Pectoral Sandpiper**, *Calidris melanotos*
183. **Sharp-tailed Sandpiper**, *Calidris acuminata*

184. **Curlew Sandpiper**, *Calidris ferruginea*
185. **Stilt Sandpiper**, *Calidris himantopus*
186. **Purple Sandpiper**, *Calidris maritima*
187. **Dunlin**, *Calidris alpina*
188. **Broad-billed Sandpiper**, *Limicola falcinellus*
189. **Buff-breasted Sandpiper**, *Tryngites subruficollis*
190. **Ruff**, *Philomachus pugnax*
191. **Jack Snipe**, *Lymnocryptes minimus*
192. **Common Snipe**, *Gallinago gallinago*
193. ***Wilson's Snipe**, *Gallinago delicata*
194. **Great Snipe**, *Gallinago media*
195. **Short-billed Dowitcher**, *Limnodromus griseus*
196. **Long-billed Dowitcher**, *Limnodromus scolopaceus*
197. **Eurasian Woodcock**, *Scolopax rusticola*
198. **Black-tailed Godwit**, *Limosa limosa*
199. **Bar-tailed Godwit**, *Limosa lapponica*
200. **Whimbrel**, *Numenius phaeopus*
201. **Eurasian Curlew**, *Numenius arquata*
202. **Upland Sandpiper**, *Bartramia longicauda*
203. **Spotted Redshank**, *Tringa erythropus*
204. **Common Redshank**, *Tringa totanus*
205. **Marsh Sandpiper**, *Tringa stagnatilis*
206. **Common Greenshank**, *Tringa nebularia*
207. **Greater Yellowlegs**, *Tringa melanoleuca*
208. **Lesser Yellowlegs**, *Tringa flavipes*
209. **Solitary Sandpiper**, *Tringa solitaria*
210. **Green Sandpiper**, *Tringa ochropus*
211. **Wood Sandpiper**, *Tringa glareola*
212. **Terek Sandpiper**, *Xenus cinereus*
213. **Common Sandpiper**, *Actitis hypoleucos*
214. **Spotted Sandpiper**, *Actitis macularius*
215. **Ruddy Turnstone**, *Arenaria interpres*
216. **Wilson's Phalarope**, *Phalaropus tricolor*
217. **Red-necked Phalarope**, *Phalaropus lobatus*
218. **Grey Phalarope**, *Phalaropus fulicarius*
219. **Pomarine Skua**, *Stercorarius pomarinus*
220. **Arctic Skua**, *Stercorarius parasiticus*

221. **Long-tailed Skua**, *Stercorarius longicaudus*
222. **Great Skua**, *Stercorarius skua*
223. **Mediterranean Gull**, *Larus melanocephalus*
224. **Laughing Gull**, *Larus atricilla*
225. **Franklin's Gull**, *Larus pipixcan*
226. **Little Gull**, *Larus minutus*
227. **Sabine's Gull**, *Larus sabini*
228. **Bonaparte's Gull**, *Larus philadelphia*
229. **Black-headed Gull**, *Larus ridibundus*
230. **Audouin's Gull**, *Larus audouinii*
231. **Ring-billed Gull**, *Larus delawarensis*
232. **Mew (Common) Gull**, *Larus canus*
233. **Lesser Black-backed Gull**, *Larus fuscus*
234. **Yellow-legged Gull**, *Larus michahellis*
235. ***North American Herring Gull**, *Larus smithsonianus*
236. **Herring Gull**, *Larus argentatus*
237. ***Caspian Gull**, *Larus cachinnans*
238. **Iceland Gull**, *Larus glaucoides*
239. **Glaucous Gull**, *Larus hyperboreus*
240. **Great Black-backed Gull**, *Larus marinus*
241. **Ross's Gull**, *Rhodostethia rosea*
242. **Black-legged Kittiwake**, *Rissa tridactyla*
243. **Ivory Gull**, *Pagophila eburnea*
244. **Sooty Tern**, *Sterna fuscata*
245. **Little Tern**, *Sterna albifrons*
246. ***Least Tern**, *Sterna antillarum*
247. **Gull-billed Tern**, *Gelochidon nilotica*
248. **Caspian Tern**, *Hydroprogne caspia*
249. **Whiskered Tern**, *Chlidonias hybrida*
250. **Black Tern**, *Chlidonias niger*
251. **White-winged Tern**, *Chlidonias leucopterus*
252. **Elegant Tern**, *Sterna elegans*
253. **Sandwich Tern**, *Sterna sandvicensis*
254. **Lesser Crested Tern**, *Sterna bengalensis*
255. **Forster's Tern**, *Sterna forsteri*
256. **Common Tern**, *Sterna hirundo*
257. **Roseate Tern**, *Sterna dougallii*
258. **Arctic Tern**, *Sterna paradisaea*
259. **Common Guillemot**, *Uria aalge*

260. **Brünnich's Guillemot**, *Uria lomvia*
261. **Razorbill**, *Alca torda*
262. **Black Guillemot**, *Cepphus grylle*
263. **Ancient Murrelet**, *Synthliboramphus antiquus*
264. **Little Auk**, *Alle alle*
265. **Atlantic Puffin**, *Fratercula arctica*
266. **Rock Pigeon**, *Columba livia*
267. **Stock Pigeon**, *Columba oenas*
268. **Common Wood Pigeon**, *Columba palumbus*
269. **Eurasian Collared Dove**, *Streptopelia decaocto*
270. **European Turtle Dove**, *Streptopelia turtur*
271. **Oriental Turtle Dove**, *Streptopelia orientalis*
272. **Rose-ringed Parakeet**, *Psittacula krameri*
273. **Great Spotted Cuckoo**, *Clamator glandarius*
274. **Common Cuckoo**, *Cuculus canorus*
275. **Yellow-billed Cuckoo**, *Coccyzus americanus*
276. **Barn Owl**, *Tyto alba*
277. **Eurasian Scops Owl**, *Otus scops*
278. **Snowy Owl**, *Bubo scandiaca*
279. **Little Owl**, *Athene noctua*
280. **Tawny Owl**, *Strix aluco*
281. **Long-eared Owl**, *Asio otus*
282. **Short-eared Owl**, *Asio flammeus*
283. **European Nightjar**, *Caprimulgus europaeus*
284. **Common Nighthawk**, *Chordeiles minor*
285. **Common Swift**, *Apus apus*
286. **Pallid Swift**, *Apus pallidus*
287. **Pacific Swift**, *Apus pacificus*
288. **Alpine Swift**, *Apus melba*
289. **Little Swift**, *Apus affinis*
290. **Common Kingfisher**, *Alcedo atthis*
291. **Belted Kingfisher**, *Ceryle alcyon*
292. **Blue-cheeked Bee-eater**, *Merops persicus*
293. **European Bee-eater**, *Merops apiaster*
294. **European Roller**, *Coracias garrulus*
295. **Hoopoe**, *Upupa epops*
296. **Eurasian Wryneck**, *Jynx torquilla*
297. **Green Woodpecker**, *Picus viridis*
298. **Great Spotted Woodpecker**, *Dendrocopos major*
299. **Lesser Spotted Woodpecker**, *Dendrocopos minor*
300. **Black Lark**, *Melanocorypha yeltoniensis*
301. **Greater Short-toed Lark**, *Calandrella brachydactyla*
302. **Wood Lark**, *Lullula arborea*

303. **Sky Lark,** *Alauda arvensis*
304. **Horned (Shore) Lark,** *Eremophila alpestris*
305. **Sand Martin,** *Riparia riparia*
306. **Purple Martin,** *Progne subis*
307. **Barn Swallow,** *Hirundo rustica*
308. **House Martin,** *Delichon urbicum*
309. **Red-rumped Swallow,** *Cecropis daurica*
310. **Cliff Swallow,** *Petrochelidon pyrrhonota*
311. **Richard's Pipit,** *Anthus richardi*
312. **Blyth's Pipit,** *Anthus godlewskii*
313. **Tawny Pipit,** *Anthus campestris*
314. **Olive-backed Pipit,** *Anthus hodgsoni*
315. **Tree Pipit,** *Anthus trivialis*
316. **Pechora Pipit,** *Anthus gustavi*
317. **Meadow Pipit,** *Anthus pratensis*
318. **Red-throated Pipit,** *Anthus cervinus*
319. **Rock Pipit,** *Anthus petrosus*
320. **Water Pipit,** *Anthus spinoletta*
321. **Buff-bellied Pipit,** *Anthus rubescens*
322. **Yellow Wagtail,** *Motacilla flava*
323. *****Black-headed Wagtail,** *Motacilla feldegg*
324. **Citrine Wagtail,** *Motacilla citreola*
325. **Grey Wagtail,** *Motacilla cinerea*
326. **White Wagtail,** *Motacilla alba*
327. *****Pied Wagtail,** *Motacilla yarellii*
328. **Cedar Waxwing,** *Bombycilla cedrorum*
329. **Bohemian Waxwing,** *Bombycilla garrulus*
330. **White-throated Dipper,** *Cinclus cinclus*
331. **Winter Wren,** *Troglodytes troglodytes*
332. **Gray Catbird,** *Dumetella carolinensis*
333. **Hedge Accentor (Dunnock),** *Prunella modularis*
334. **Alpine Accentor,** *Prunella collaris*
335. **European Robin,** *Erithacus rubecula*
336. **Thrush Nightingale,** *Luscinia luscinia*
337. **Common Nightingale,** *Luscinia megarhynchos*
338. **Siberian Rubythroat,** *Luscinia calliope*
339. **Bluethroat,** *Luscinia svecica*
340. **Red-flanked Bluetail,** *Tarsiger cyanurus*

341. **Black Redstart,** *Phoenicurus ochruros*
342. **Common Redstart,** *Phoenicurus phoenicurus*
343. **Whinchat,** *Saxicola rubetra*
344. **Stonechat,** *Saxicola torquata*
345. ***Siberian Stonechat,** *Saxicola maura*
346. **Isabelline Wheatear,** *Oenanthe isabellina*
347. **Northern Wheatear,** *Oenanthe oenanthe*
348. **Pied Wheatear,** *Oenanthe pleschanka*
349. **Black-eared Wheatear,** *Oenanthe hispanica*
350. **Desert Wheatear,** *Oenanthe deserti*
351. **Rufous-tailed Rock Thrush,** *Monticola saxatilis*
352. **White's Thrush,** *Zoothera dauma*
353. **Swainson's Thrush,** *Catharus ustulatus*
354. **Grey-cheeked Thrush,** *Catharus minimus*
355. **Ring Ouzel,** *Turdus torquatus*
356. **Common Blackbird,** *Turdus merula*
357. **Naumann's Thrush,** *Turdus naumanni*
358. **Red-throated Thrush,** *Turdus ruficollis*
359. ***Black-throated Thrush,** *Turdus atrogularis*
360. **Fieldfare,** *Turdus pilaris*
361. **Song Thrush,** *Turdus philomelos*
362. **Redwing,** *Turdus iliacus*
363. **Mistle Thrush,** *Turdus viscivorus*
364. **American Robin,** *Turdus migratorius*
365. **Cetti's Warbler,** *Cettia cetti*
366. **Pallas's Grasshopper Warbler,** *Locustella certhiola*
367. **Lanceolated Warbler,** *Locustella lanceolata*
368. **Common Grasshopper Warbler,** *Locustella naevia*
369. **River Warbler,** *Locustella fluviatilis*
370. **Savi's Warbler,** *Locustella luscinioides*
371. **Aquatic Warbler,** *Acrocephalus paludicola*
372. **Sedge Warbler,** *Acrocephalus schoenobaenus*
373. **Paddyfield Warbler,** *Acrocephalus agricola*
374. **Blyth's Reed Warbler,** *Acrocephalus dumetorum*
375. **Marsh Warbler,** *Acrocephalus palustris*
376. **Eurasian Reed Warbler,** *Acrocephalus scirpaceus*
377. **Great Reed Warbler,** *Acrocephalus arundinaceus*
378. **Eastern Olivaceous Warbler,** *Hippolais pallida*

379. **Booted Warbler**, *Hippolais caligata*
380. **Icterine Warbler**, *Hippolais icterina*
381. **Melodious Warbler**, *Hippolais polyglotta*
382. **Blackcap**, *Sylvia atricapilla*
383. **Garden Warbler**, *Sylvia borin*
384. **Barred Warbler**, *Sylvia nisoria*
385. **Lesser Whitethroat**, *Sylvia curruca*
386. ***Desert Lesser Whitethroat**, *Sylvia minula*
387. **Asian Desert Warbler**, *Sylvia nana*
388. **Common Whitethroat**, *Sylvia communis*
389. **Spectacled Warbler**, *Sylvia conspicillata*
390. ***Eastern Subalpine Warbler**, *Sylvia albistriata*
391. **Western Subalpine Warbler**, *Sylvia cantillans*
392. **Dartford Warbler**, *Sylvia undata*
393. **Marmora's Warbler**, *Sylvia sarda*
394. **Rüppell's Warbler**, *Sylvia rueppelli*
395. **Sardinian Warbler**, *Sylvia melanocephala*
396. **Greenish Warbler**, *Phylloscopus trochiloides*
397. ***Two-barred Greenish Warbler**, *Phylloscopus plumbeitarsus*
398. **Arctic Warbler**, *Phylloscopus borealis*
399. **Pallas's Leaf Warbler**, *Phylloscopus proregulus*
400. **Yellow-browed Warbler**, *Phylloscopus inornatus*
401. **Hume's Leaf Warbler**, *Phylloscopus humei*
402. **Radde's Warbler**, *Phylloscopus schwarzi*
403. **Dusky Warbler**, *Phylloscopus fuscatus*
404. **Western Bonelli's Warbler**, *Phylloscopus bonelli*
405. **Wood Warbler**, *Phylloscopus sibilatrix*
406. **Common Chiffchaff**, *Phylloscopus collybita*
407. **Iberian Chiffchaff**, *Phylloscopus ibericus*
408. ***Siberian Chiffchaff**, *Phylloscopus tristis*
409. **Willow Warbler**, *Phylloscopus trochilus*
410. **Goldcrest**, *Regulus regulus*
411. **Firecrest**, *Regulus ignicapilla*
412. **Spotted Flycatcher**, *Muscicapa striata*
413. **Red-breasted Flycatcher**, *Ficedula parva*
414. **Taiga Flycatcher**, *Ficedula albicilla*

415. **Collared Flycatcher,** *Ficedula albicollis*
416. **Pied Flycatcher,** *Ficedula hypoleuca*
417. **Bearded Tit,** *Panurus biarmicus*
418. **Long-tailed Tit,** *Aegithalos caudatus*
419. **Blue Tit,** *Cyanistes caeruleus*
420. **Great Tit,** *Parus major*
421. **Crested Tit,** *Lophophanes cristatus*
422. **Coal Tit,** *Parus ater*
423. **Willow Tit,** *Parus montanus*
424. **Marsh Tit,** *Parus palustris*
425. **Red-breasted Nuthatch,** *Sitta canadensis*
426. **Wood Nuthatch,** *Sitta europaea*
427. **Eurasian Treecreeper,** *Certhia familiaris*
428. **Short-toed Treecreeper,** *Certhia brachydactyla*
429. **Eurasian Penduline Tit,** *Remiz pendulinus*
430. **Eurasian Golden Oriole,** *Oriolus oriolus*
431. **Isabelline Shrike,** *Lanius isabellinus*
432. **Red-backed Shrike,** *Lanius collurio*
433. **Lesser Grey Shrike,** *Lanius minor*
434. **Great Grey Shrike,** *Lanius excubitor*
435. **Southern Grey Shrike,** *Lanius meridionalis*
436. **Woodchat Shrike,** *Lanius senator*
437. **Masked Shrike,** *Lanius nubicus*
438. **Eurasian Jay,** *Garrulus glandarius*
439. **Black-billed Magpie,** *Pica pica*
440. **Spotted Nutcracker,** *Nucifraga caryocatactes*
441. **Red-billed Chough,** *Pyrrhocorax pyrrhocorax*
442. **Eurasian Jackdaw,** *Corvus monedula*
443. **Rook,** *Corvus frugilegus*
444. **Carrion Crow,** *Corvus corone*
445. **Hooded Crow,** *Corvus cornix*
446. **Common Raven,** *Corvus corax*
447. **Common Starling,** *Sturnus vulgaris*
448. **Rosy Starling,** *Sturnus roseus*
449. **House Sparrow,** *Passer domesticus*
450. **Spanish Sparrow,** *Passer hispaniolensis*
451. **Eurasian Tree Sparrow,** *Passer montanus*
452. **Yellow-throated Vireo,** *Vireo flavifrons*
453. **Red-eyed Vireo,** *Vireo olivaceus*

454. **Chaffinch**, *Fringilla coelebs*
455. **Brambling**, *Fringilla montifringilla*
456. **European Serin**, *Serinus serinus*
457. **European Greenfinch**, *Carduelis chloris*
458. **European Goldfinch**, *Carduelis carduelis*
459. **Eurasian Siskin**, *Carduelis spinus*
460. **Common Linnet**, *Carduelis cannabina*
461. **Twite**, *Carduelis flavirostris*
462. **Lesser Redpoll**, *Carduelis cabaret*
463. **Common Redpoll**, *Carduelis flammea*
464. **Arctic Redpoll**, *Carduelis hornemanni*
465. ***Northwestern Redpoll**, *Carduelis rostrata*
466. **Two-barred Crossbill**, *Loxia leucoptera*
467. **Common Crossbill**, *Loxia curvirostra*
468. **Parrot Crossbill**, *Loxia pytyopsittacus*
469. **Trumpeter Finch**, *Bucanetes githagineus*
470. **Common Rosefinch**, *Carpodacus erythrinus*
471. **Pine Grosbeak**, *Pinicola enucleator*
472. **Common Bullfinch**, *Pyrrhula pyrrhula*
473. **Hawfinch**, *Coccothraustes coccothraustes*
474. **Black-and-white Warbler**, *Mniotilta varia*
475. **Golden-winged Warbler**, *Vermivora chrysoptera*
476. **Blue-winged Warbler (IRBC)**, *Vermivora pinus*
477. **Yellow Warbler**, *Dendroica petechia*
478. **Yellow-rumped Warbler**, *Dendroica coronata*
479. **Blackpoll Warbler**, *Dendroica striata*
480. **Ovenbird**, *Seiurus aurocapilla*
481. **Northern Waterthrush**, *Seiurus noveboracensis*
482. **Common Yellowthroat**, *Geothlypis trichas*
483. **Lark Sparrow**, *Chondestes grammacus*
484. **Savannah Sparrow**, *Passerculus sandwichensis*
485. **Song Sparrow**, *Melospiza melodia*
486. **White-crowned Sparrow**, *Zonotrichia leucophrys*
487. **White-throated Sparrow**, *Zonotrichia albicollis*
488. **Dark-eyed Junco**, *Junco hyemalis*
489. **Lapland Longspur**, *Calcarius lapponicus*
490. **Snow Bunting**, *Plectrophenax nivalis*

491. **Black-faced Bunting**, *Emberiza spodocephala*
492. **Pine Bunting**, *Emberiza leucocephalos*
493. **Yellowhammer**, *Emberiza citrinella*
494. **Cirl Bunting**, *Emberiza cirlus*
495. **Ortolan Bunting**, *Emberiza hortulana*
496. **Yellow-browed Bunting**, *Emberiza chrysophrys*
497. ***Chestnut-eared Bunting**, *Emberiza fucata*
498. **Rustic Bunting**, *Emberiza rustica*
499. **Little Bunting**, *Emberiza pusilla*
500. **Yellow-breasted Bunting**, *Emberiza aureola*
501. **Reed Bunting**, *Emberiza schoeniclus*
502. **Black-headed Bunting**, *Emberiza melanocephala*
503. **Corn Bunting**, *Emberiza calandra*
504. **Indigo Bunting**, *Passerina cyanea*
505. **Bobolink**, *Dolichonyx oryzivorus*
506. **Baltimore Oriole**, *Icterus galbula*

Online Resources for Birders

Information services & birding websites

Bird Information Service
www.birdingworld.co.uk
Birding World *magazine and* Birdline, *the premium rate rare bird news service*

Birdguides
www.birdguides.com
Birding resources online including latest sightings and text alerts, photos and site guide

Birdnet
www.birdnet.co.uk
Rare bird information including paging services; photos, books and optics

Rare Bird Alert
www.rarebirdalert.co.uk
Rare bird information including paging services; online photos and written articles

Surfbirds
www.surfbirds.com
Birding resources online, including photo galleries, forums, sketchbooks, written articles and trip reports

Fatbirder
www.fatbirder.com
Online birding resources. Has an especially useful comprehensive list of links to recommended websites.

UK400Club
www.uk400clubonline.co.uk
Resource specifically for those interested in rare birds in Britain and Ireland; website contains written articles by Lee Evans and league tables of birders and their lists, with associated guidelines on what to count

British Birds Rarities Committee
www.bbrc.org.uk
Official vetting committee for the submission of sightings of rare birds in Britain

British Ornithologists' Union
www.bou.org.uk
Promotion of bird study for the advancement of science and to aid conservation

The British Trust for Ornithology
www.bto.org

Conservation

The Royal Society for the Protection of Birds
www.rspb.org.uk

The Wildlife Trusts
www.wildlifetrusts.org

Birdlife International
www.birdlife.net

Glossary

Bins: Binoculars

Birder: Someone who has a keen interest in, and who watches birds regularly, hence birding. 'Twitching' can be described as one form of 'birding'.

Blocker: An exceptionally rare bird, not having been seen in one's home country, at least by the masses, for a number of years. Slang such as 'megacrippler' or 'stonker' are occasionally used to represent an extreme rarity, particularly one that 'shows well'.

Connecting: Gaining visual contact with the bird. Sometimes described as 'getting onto' the bird particularly if, for whatever reason, it is proving difficult to see.

Crippling views: Good views of a bird. Such a bird is said to be 'showing well.'

Dip: A failed attempt to see a bird; hence dipped/dipping. 'Negative news' means the bird hasn't been seen.

Dude: Someone with a more casual interest in birdwatching. Very rarely referred to as a 'robin-stroker'.

Mega: An exceptionally rare bird. Pagers have a 'mega alert' which overrides the countless less intrusive alerts detailing sightings of more common birds.

Mega-mover: Someone who is willing to travel anywhere in the country at the drop of a hat for a rarity. Like the birds themselves, mega-movers usually fly and are referred to by some as 'chequebook birders' (for obvious reasons). Some get edgy if placed too far away from an airport during the critical month of October.

String: A dubious claim of a bird (hence 'stringer').

Twitcher: A term grossly over-used by the press to describe anyone with any kind of a link to birds. The word really refers to someone who travels to see a specific rare or scarce bird at a given locality. Rarely used by 'twitchers' themselves, although I use the term to differentiate this type of birder from the 'non-twitching' type.

Acknowledgements

My sincere thanks to all those who have accompanied me on my various quests to see birds, particularly the drivers. Thanks are especially due to Adrian and Dave Webb, who more than once have shown an exceptional ability to stay alert whilst driving long distances and to Adrian for his excellent photographs, some of which I have included in this book; also to Paul Doherty for allowing me to use his crowd shot taken in Kent; to the finders of the rare birds, without whom this book would not have been possible, and to those who help 'spread the word'; to Nicola and Hugh Loxdale of Brambleby Books for all their hard work in helping me realise my dream of getting this book into production; to Adrian Riley and John Oates for their editing skills and sound advice on the text contained within; and to John and other Cambs birders, notably Jim Lawrence and Mark Hawkes, for keeping me updated with local developments; to Steve Gent for keeping me informed; to my girlfriend Liz for not only proofreading the manuscript, but for always showing an exceptional degree of patience (even during the madness that was October 2004) and for not complaining once, even when I 'hijacked' our holiday in Scotland by going to see a duck in the Outer Hebrides; and more especially to my long-suffering mother whose unwavering love and support means everything to me,…as did her car and chauffeuring service while I was still in my teens. She has given me much throughout sometimes difficult times, and I am eternally grateful. Lastly, I wish to give a big 'thank you' to all conservation workers everywhere for their invaluable work which ensures that the birds which we observe and revere will – hopefully – continue to thrive for a long time yet to come.

Other bird books from Brambleby Books

Bird Words – Poetic images of wild birds
Hugh David Loxdale
ISBN: 0954334736, 80pp., £5.99

'A paperback of poems by a poet and professional biologist, reminding us that wild birds continue to inspire and delight in a host of different ways.'
Rob Hume, *RSPB*, 2004

Arrivals and Rivals: a birding oddity
Adrian Riley
ISBN: 0954334760, 165pp., £7.99

'While the romance of Adrian's quest is highly readable, it is the Rivals part that makes it so addictive...Even non-birders who question what makes grown men sacrifice so much for often a fleeting glimpse of a bird as it flies away will find many of their questions answered.'
Stuart Winter, *Sunday Express*, June 12th, 2005

Feathers and Eggshells – The Bird Journal of a Young London Girl
Natalie Lawrence
ISBN: 0954334779, 71pp., £15.50

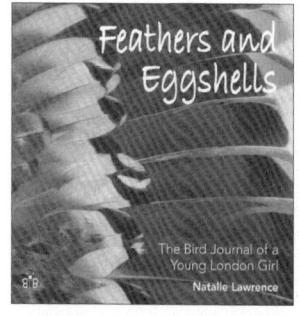

'Once you have opened its pages, you will probably want to own a copy or better still buy it as a present for a young birdwatcher that you know... This is an extraordinary book – a remarkable achievement by a sixteen year old girl, who has clearly had a passion for natural history since a very young age.... I absolutely loved everything about this book and only wish that it had been around to inspire me as a young teenager.'
Jenny Steel, www.haiths.com, 2006